An Analysis of

John Locke's

Two Treatises of Government

Jeremy Kleidosty
with
Ian Jackson

Published by Macat International Ltd
24:13 Coda Centre, 189 Munster Road, London SW6 6AW.

Distributed exclusively by Routledge
2 Park Square, Milton Park, Abingdon, Oxon OX14 4RN
711 Third Avenue, New York, NY 10017, USA

Routledge is an imprint of the Taylor & Francis Group, an informa business

www.macat.com
info@macat.com

Cataloguing in Publication Data
A catalogue record for this book is available from the British Library.
Library of Congress Cataloguing-in-Publication Data is available upon request.
Cover illustration: Etienne Gilfillan

ISBN 978-1-912303-35-9 (hardback)
ISBN 978-1-912127-55-9 (paperback)
ISBN 978-1-912282-23-4 (e-book)

Notice
The information in this book is designed to orientate readers of the work under analysis,
to elucidate and contextualise its key ideas and themes, and to aid in the development
of critical thinking skills. It is not meant to be used, nor should it be used, as a
substitute for original thinking or in place of original writing or research. References and
notes are provided for informational purposes and their presence does not constitute
endorsement of the information or opinions therein. This book is presented solely for
educational purposes. It is sold on the understanding that the publisher is not engaged
to provide any scholarly advice. The publisher has made every effort to ensure that
this book is accurate and up-to-date, but makes no warranties or representations with
regard to the completeness or reliability of the information it contains. The information
and the opinions provided herein are not guaranteed or warranted to produce particular
results and may not be suitable for students of every ability. The publisher shall not be
liable for any loss, damage or disruption arising from any errors or omissions, or from
the use of this book, including, but not limited to, special, incidental, consequential or
other damages caused, or alleged to have been caused, directly or indirectly, by the
information contained within.

CONTENTS

THE MACAT LIBRARY

The Macat Library is a series of unique academic explorations of seminal works in the humanities and social sciences – books and papers that have had a significant and widely recognised impact on their disciplines. It has been created to serve as much more than just a summary of what lies between the covers of a great book. It illuminates and explores the influences on, ideas of, and impact of that book. Our goal is to offer a learning resource that encourages critical thinking and fosters a better, deeper understanding of important ideas.

Each publication is divided into three Sections: Influences, Ideas, and Impact. Each Section has four Modules. These explore every important facet of the work, and the responses to it.

This Section-Module structure makes a Macat Library book easy to use, but it has another important feature. Because each Macat book is written to the same format, it is possible (and encouraged!) to cross-reference multiple Macat books along the same lines of inquiry or research. This allows the reader to open up interesting interdisciplinary pathways.

To further aid your reading, lists of glossary terms and people mentioned are included at the end of this book (these are indicated by an asterisk [*] throughout) – as well as a list of works cited.

Macat has worked with the University of Cambridge to identify the elements of critical thinking and understand the ways in which six different skills combine to enable effective thinking.
Three allow us to fully understand a problem; three more give us the tools to solve it. Together, these six skills make up the **PACIER** model of critical thinking. They are:

ANALYSIS – understanding how an argument is built
EVALUATION – exploring the strengths and weaknesses of an argument
INTERPRETATION – understanding issues of meaning

CREATIVE THINKING – coming up with new ideas and fresh connections
PROBLEM-SOLVING – producing strong solutions
REASONING – creating strong arguments

To find out more, visit **WWW.MACAT.COM.**

CRITICAL THINKING AND
TWO TREATISES OF GOVERNMENT

Primary critical thinking skill: EVALUATION
Secondary critical thinking skill: REASONING

John Locke's 1689 *Two Treatises of Government* is a key text in the history of political theory – one whose influence remains marked on modern politics, the American Constitution and beyond.

Two Treatises is more than a seminal work on the nature and legitimacy of government. It is also a masterclass in two key critical thinking skills: evaluation and reasoning. Evaluation is all about judging and assessing arguments – asking how relevant, adequate and convincing they are. And, at its heart, the first of Locke's two treatises is pure evaluation: a long and incisive dissection of a treatise on the arguments in Sir Robert Filmer's Patriarcha. Filmer's book had defended the doctrine that kings were absolute rulers whose legitimacy came directly from God (the so-called "divine right of kings"), basing his arguments on Biblical explanations and evidence. Locke carefully rebutted Filmer's arguments, on their own terms, by reference to both the Bible and to recorded history. Finding Filmer's evidence either to be insufficient or unacceptable, Locke concluded that his argument for patriarchy was weak to the point of invalidity.

In the second of Locke's treatises, the author goes on to construct his own argument concerning the sources of legitimate power, and the nature of that power. Carefully building his own argument from a logical consideration of man in "the state of nature", Locke creates a convincing argument that civilised society should be based on natural human rights and the social contract.

ABOUT THE AUTHOR OF THE ORIGINAL WORK

English political philosopher **John Locke** is considered one of the most important thinkers of the Enlightenment era. Born into a well-off English family in 1632, he rose to work for a series of highly influential men, and even the government. His ideas about men's inalienable rights and what makes for a legitimate government have had a profound impact on Western political and philosophical thinking. Locke never married or had children, and died in 1704 at the age of 72.

ABOUT THE AUTHOR OF THE ANALYSIS

Dr Jeremy Kleidosty received his PhD in international relations from the University of St Andrews. He is currently a postdoctoral fellow at the University of Jväskylä, and is the author of *The Concert of Civilizations: The Common Roots of Western and Islamic Constitutionalism.*

Ian Jackson is a PhD student in the Politics, Philosophy and Religion department at Lancaster University. He is interested in the role new media plays in the dissemination of ideas.

ABOUT MACAT

GREAT WORKS FOR CRITICAL THINKING

Macat is focused on making the ideas of the world's great thinkers accessible and comprehensible to everybody, everywhere, in ways that promote the development of enhanced critical thinking skills.

It works with leading academics from the world's top universities to produce new analyses that focus on the ideas and the impact of the most influential works ever written across a wide variety of academic disciplines. Each of the works that sit at the heart of its growing library is an enduring example of great thinking. But by setting them in context – and looking at the influences that shaped their authors, as well as the responses they provoked – Macat encourages readers to look at these classics and game-changers with fresh eyes. Readers learn to think, engage and challenge their ideas, rather than simply accepting them.

'Macat offers an amazing first-of-its-kind tool for interdisciplinary learning and research. Its focus on works that transformed their disciplines and its rigorous approach, drawing on the world's leading experts and educational institutions, opens up a world-class education to anyone.'

Andreas Schleicher
Director for Education and Skills, Organisation for Economic
Co-operation and Development

'Macat is taking on some of the major challenges in university education … They have drawn together a strong team of active academics who are producing teaching materials that are novel in the breadth of their approach.'

Prof Lord Broers,
former Vice-Chancellor of the University of Cambridge

'The Macat vision is exceptionally exciting. It focuses upon new modes of learning which analyse and explain seminal texts which have profoundly influenced world thinking and so social and economic development. It promotes the kind of critical thinking which is essential for any society and economy. This is the learning of the future.'

Rt Hon Charles Clarke, former UK Secretary of State for Education

'The Macat analyses provide immediate access to the critical conversation surrounding the books that have shaped their respective discipline, which will make them an invaluable resource to all of those, students and teachers, working in the field.'

Professor William Tronzo, University of California at San Diego

WAYS IN TO THE TEXT

KEY POINTS

- John Locke was an English philosopher born in 1632.

- In *Two Treatises of Government*, he argues that it was not God who put the king in charge of ruling the country—it was the people.

- Locke's ideas, radical for the time, began the political philosophy known as classical liberalism.*

Who was John Locke?

John Locke, the author of *Two Treatises of Government*, was born on August 26, 1632, in the English county of Somerset. His father, a lawyer, had been a captain in the parliamentarian army during the English Civil War*—a conflict fought between supporters of a monarchy* headed by King Charles I* and supporters of a system of government where power lay in parliament.* Thanks to his position, he was able to send his son to the prestigious Westminster School in London.

From there, Locke went to Oxford University, where he gained a bachelor's degree in 1656. Further study led to a master's degree in 1658, and a degree in medicine in 1674. After university, Locke worked as a doctor for the Earl of Shaftesbury,* an influential politician of the time. Locke also went to France to work as a doctor, and later gained some experience of international trade by working for the English government.

The Civil War in England lasted from 1642 to 1651 and caused many to ask questions about what kind of government was best for the country. Two men in particular, the political theorist Robert Filmer* and the philosopher Thomas Hobbes,* arrived at a similar answer: only a king could make sure that everyone in society behaved themselves, they believed, and the king was given his power by God— meaning that his right to rule was divine.* Locke disagreed, and wrote *Two Treatises* as a counterargument sometime between 1679 and 1689, when it was published anonymously, mainly because his ideas were so clearly controversial.

In 1683, Locke had himself been implicated in the Rye House Plot,* a plan to kill the current king, Charles II.* Despite being a Protestant,* Charles had some sympathy with Roman Catholics.* Indeed, his brother James* was one. The Rye House Plotters were Protestants who were staunchly anti-Catholic and feared that the country would once more be ruled by a Roman Catholic when Charles died, because he had no heir and as such his brother James would become king. By killing Charles they believed they would be able to halt the return of Roman Catholics to the throne. Locke's involvement had been to arrange accommodation for one of the main plotters. However, the plot failed, and as Charles cracked down on hardcore Protestants, Locke was forced to flee to the Netherlands and to stay there until a new king, William III,* took control of England in what is today known as the Glorious Revolution of 1688.*

What Does *Two Treatises* Say?

Although most countries in the world were then ruled by some kind of monarch, there had been very little thought given to explaining why. The question of where power resided in a state, however, became a particularly important question in the United Kingdom, where there had been bloody conflict over the extent of the king's power.

King Charles I was executed in 1649 and the Civil War had been costly for England as a whole. Because it was a recent memory, it provided an important context for Locke's political work. By the time he wrote his *Two Treatises*, King Charles's son, Charles II, was on the throne, and the old question of how much power the king should have was being asked again.

Some thought the war proved the need for a strong king to keep order. Thinkers like Filmer and Hobbes, for example, were convinced that without a king the country would fall to pieces. Locke begins *Two Treatises of Government* by arguing with Filmer over the origin of kingly power. For Locke, the king's right to rule does not come from God, but from the people he rules. And Locke does not write about what is best for the people of England alone. He couches his argument as universal—that is, as concerning the rights of all people, everywhere.

He uses the language of the Bible, of science, and even of Hobbes, somebody whose opinions he did not share. Locke does not spend much time in *Two Treatises* talking about real history. Instead he turns to an invented, speculative history to explain his view of society.

In his view, people start out living in what he calls the "state of nature."* Society began, he argues, so that people could decide who owned property. The idea of property is important to Locke since he believes that in the state of nature everything was free and nobody owned anything. But if that were true, Locke asks, how did the idea of property come about?

His answer begins with the argument that, once, people could take what they wanted as long as they left behind enough for anyone else that might need it. While human beings were still few in number, this was not a problem. But as land and resources became harder to find, the idea of leaving behind enough for everyone to enjoy was no longer possible. Some people worked hard to make the best use of what they had, Locke argues. A farmer, for example, mixed his labor with the soil to produce more than would grow if the food grew wild—and this was the germ of the idea of ownership.

The problem of property was that anyone could steal it. So laws to protect property from thieves became important. Laws, of course, have to be upheld, and so people needed some form of government to make sure that everyone followed the new rules. For much of human history, this meant having a king who could keep order in society.

Locke's innovation is to describe this as a kind of contract. Although people still had rights, they gave some of them away in return for the king's protection. The king would make sure that people behaved in a respectful way to each other—but, as far as Locke is concerned, that doesn't mean that the king is above the law. The contract works both ways. If the king does not obey the law, then somebody else should rule.

Why Does *Two Treatises* Matter?

Locke's ideas, describing a society different from the one in which most people lived, were revolutionary. He felt that the people should have some say in who ran the country. If a government did not work in the interests of the people, he supported the idea of rebellion against it.

After Locke's death in 1704, many important thinkers, among them the Scottish philosopher David Hume,* expanded on his ideas. By the eighteenth century they were in common circulation. The American War of Independence,* fought by 13 of Britain's colonies* against the British between 1775 and 1783, was founded on Locke's idea that people need not obey a bad government. Many of the men involved in the revolution, among them the political theorist Thomas Paine* and the statesman Thomas Jefferson,* supported Locke's ideas. When the colonies won the war, they created a type of government similar to the one Locke had argued for, where there was no king, where there were elections, and where the government protected people's rights.

Today, these liberal* ideas do not seem controversial. Thanks to

Locke, liberalism has become one of the most successful political movements of all time. Notions that started in Europe during the period known as the Enlightenment,* marked by a move towards rational thought, found a home in the young United States, where it was proven that a liberal state would not fall into chaos as men like Hobbes had warned. It was a radical time; in France the people put on trial and executed a king who had, until then, enjoyed something close to absolute power, instituting a republic of their own.

Those living in a liberal democracy* today enjoy a system of government that owes something to Locke's ideas. The influential US Constitution,* for example, a document written to describe and guarantee the rights of American citizens, was based on Locke's philosophy. It continues to be relevant to American politics now.

Today, when people suspect their government is growing powerful at the expense of their liberty—threatening a right such as free speech or privacy, for example—Locke's ideas can still be useful. Although many important thinkers have modified and added to his ideas, it is Locke who is considered the father of classical liberalism. Without *Two Treatises*, the world around us would be a very different place.

SECTION 1
INFLUENCES

MODULE 1
THE AUTHOR AND THE HISTORICAL CONTEXT

KEY POINTS

- *Two Treatises of Government* is one of the greatest works ever written in political philosophy and had a clear influence long after John Locke's death in 1704.

- Locke was a privileged member of society and received what was for the time an excellent education.

- An attempt had been made in England to govern the country without a king. Though of limited success, it had been no *less* successful than monarchy had been, and had therefore inspired questions about which system was best.

Why Read this Text?

There is considerable debate over the originality of many of John Locke's ideas in *Two Treatises of Government*. It is, however, generally agreed that his formulation of the evolution of property rights* and their relation to the creation and functions of the state is a major contribution to political thought.[1] Furthermore, his original and influential work on when it is acceptable to rebel against authority had a direct effect on the tumultuous political landscape of the eighteenth century.[2]

Although *Two Treatises* is a work that attempts to justify many of the ideologies and political actions of its time, it does so without completely agreeing with or rejecting any dominant school of thought. It may even be seen as contradictory in its justification of colonialism,* while rejecting tyranny and calling for rebellion against it.[3]

> ❝ There is land enough in the world to suffice double the inhabitants had not the invention of money, and the tacit agreement of men to put a value on it, introduced (by consent) larger possessions. ❞
> John Locke, *Two Treatises of Government*

What is clear, however, is that its influence stretched well beyond Locke's lifetime. As a work that inspired the creation of the American state and influenced key thinkers such as the radical political theorist Thomas Paine,* the philosopher David Hume,* and the political philosopher Jean-Jacques Rousseau,* it remains one of political philosophy's greatest works. Any attempt to understand the evolution of Western political thought is incomplete without an appreciation of Locke's ideas and the ways in which they were later implemented into working political systems.

Author's Life
Locke's father was an English lawyer with a small amount of property. He got his son into a good school, where he did well enough to be accepted into Oxford University. At Oxford, Locke studied politics, medicine, and science more generally.[4] Although well educated and part of the political class, it was his association with more powerful men such as the First Earl of Shaftesbury,* a politician of some influence, that was to define his career.

It is impossible to disentangle the message of Locke's text from the influences of his social and educational background, and from his circle of close friends and colleagues. The religious and civil conflicts that England had endured from the mid-seventeenth century onwards had greatly destabilized the country. Virtually everyone in the political class was forced to choose sides between the Roman Catholic* and Protestant* Christian doctrines, between republican* and monarchist,* and so on.

Locke's background as the son of a Protestant and his education at Westminster School in London and Oxford University led him to seek a history of the state that explained its origins in nature and society.[5] This was an account that undermined religious justifications for the legitimacy of the power of a monarch or government. This history of the state would also allow him to justify colonialism and to explain property rights, which were central concerns in a time of imperial expansion and increased capitalism.*

Although Locke never pretended to be consistent in terms of his philosophy, or to belong to any particular school of thought, his association with Shaftesbury substantially colored his view of politics specifically, and of the world more generally. Through Shaftesbury, Locke participated in pivotal events such as the running of the Carolina colony (now the American states of North and South Carolina) and in what historians call the "exclusion crises."* These were the political attempts to prevent the future King James II,* a Roman Catholic, from succeeding his brother Charles II,* a Protestant, to the throne. Locke genuinely seemed to fear that a Roman Catholic king would plunge the largely Protestant state into renewed religious war.[6]

It seems unlikely that such a text as *Two Treatises* could have been completed by anyone else at any other time. It legitimized the idea of questioning the divine right of kings*—the notion that a monarch's power came from God—in a quite unprecedented way.

Author's Background

The context in which Locke wrote the *Two Treatises* has been intensely debated. While the exact date of the text—understood to be somewhere between 1679 and 1689—is unclear, the historical background itself is easier to define.

England had been without a king for some 19 years after the execution of Charles I,* but the monarchy was restored in 1660.

Although the new king, Charles II, was not welcomed by all, towards the end of his reign questions surrounding his eventual replacement came to dominate political thought. Charles II had no legitimate heir, meaning that his brother James II would be king after his death. This was unacceptable to many, as James was dictatorial, refused to cooperate with parliament,* and above all else was openly Roman Catholic.

When Charles II died in 1685, James II did indeed become king— but his reign lasted less than three years. He fled the country in 1688 and the Protestant William of Orange* and his wife Mary* were proclaimed king and queen in his place, in what has come to be known as the "Glorious Revolution."*

This all means that the text's date of publication, 1689, is significant. Questions of how a nation should best be governed were pressing as the rule of James II had failed. Locke, who had himself been falsely accused of conspiring to kill Charles II in what was known as the Rye House Plot,* had been living in exile in the Netherlands since 1683 and did not return until after the Glorious Revolution of 1688, traveling back with the future Queen Mary II herself.

Regardless of whether Locke completed *Two Treatises* earlier or later, its publication in 1689 showed that the political situation in England was far from certain.

NOTES

1   Peter Laslett, introduction to John Locke, *Two Treatises of Government*, ed. Peter Laslett, 2nd ed. (Cambridge: Cambridge University Press, 1988), 101.

2   V.C. Chappell, *The Cambridge Companion to Locke* (Cambridge: Cambridge University Press, 1994), 228.

3   See especially the second treatise, chapter 5 "Of Property" and chapter 18 "Of Tyranny," in Locke, *Two Treatises*.

4   Laslett, introduction to *Two Treatises*, 17–24.

5   Laslett, introduction to *Two Treatises*, 18–22, 40–45.

6   See David Armitage, "John Locke, Carolina, and the Two Treatises of
    Government," *Political Theory* 32, 5 (2004): 602–27; also Laslett,
    introduction to *Two Treatises*, 25–44.

MODULE 2
ACADEMIC CONTEXT

KEY POINTS

- *Two Treatises* was one of the first works to investigate the political philosophy of liberalism.*

- Throughout the period known as the Enlightenment,* a time of discussion and increasing rationality, people started to question long-held ideas about the rights of people and the power of the state.

- Locke began to look at ways in which states could potentially be run based on nature and society, rather than on religious notions about kings who had been chosen by God.

The Work In Its Context

The political philosophy of liberalism, which we can trace from John Locke's *Two Treatises of Government*, centers on a specific idea: the rights of the individual.

Since the consensus appears to be that people cannot be allowed absolute freedom to act as they please, it naturally follows that the government must retain certain powers in order to prevent anarchy,* a society where there is no government or law. While the idea of rights and freedoms is today commonplace, this was not the case when *Two Treatises* appeared in 1689. Indeed, many people felt that the king was above the law—though this may have been more the case in France than in England, as the English had enjoyed traditional civil liberties (they were subject only to laws that were agreed for the general good of the community) for some time.

The English Civil War* of 1642 to 1651 had initially been fought

> 66 This Sovereign is by no means necessarily a king. It can either be one man or an assembly of men. 99
>
> Thomas Hobbes, *Leviathan*

over the idea that Charles I* should be accountable to parliament* on the raising of taxes. But holding kings to account was an idea ahead of its time. Ultimately, Locke's views were not put into practice until after the American War of Independence,* which happened between 1775 and 1783. By that time Locke's ideas had been expanded on by thinkers such as the philosopher David Hume.*

Thanks to Locke, questions about property, tyranny, and political rebellion could for the first time be viewed as something more than abstractions. They were questions grounded in actual events that had affected the lives of many, especially in England. At the same time, Locke's highlighting of general principles helped explain how different types of government and political belief interacted with one another. As a result, his ideas were easily applied to contexts quite different from those he personally experienced.[1]

Overview of the Field

Locke wrote *Two Treatises of Government* in a context rife with political revolution* and controversy. Unsurprisingly, he was not the only thinker who had contemplated these ideas. Two important figures, Robert Filmer* and Thomas Hobbes,* had also tackled the same questions, but had arrived at very different answers.

Filmer's great *Patriarcha*, published after his death in 1680, was as much a product of the contemporary political landscape as Locke's work. Set against the background of the conflict between parliament and Charles I that ultimately led to the English Civil War, *Patriarcha* offered a biblical justification for why kings should rule. Filmer cited the model of a family where the father makes the decisions and passes this power on to his eldest son on death.[2] Though Filmer was not the only philosopher to argue in favor of the divine right of kings* (that kings had been chosen by God, and so therefore had the right to make decisions alone), Locke nonetheless singled him out. The first of the book's two treatises was, in fact, written as a direct counterargument to Filmer's ideas.

Hobbes was an altogether different character to Filmer. His 1651 book *Leviathan*, a very important work, was written during the chaotic years of the English Civil War. In it, Hobbes introduced the concept of a social contract,* which held that governments are formed when a social group agrees to be ruled by a ruler or ruling class so that their lives and certain fundamental rights can be protected. This idea implies that governments that do not fulfill their obligations are invalid.

The significance of this cannot be overstated. The social contract can be seen as the root of all modern Western political philosophy. Hobbes, like Filmer, argued in favor of the right of kings, but on practical rather than theological* grounds. Having witnessed the chaos of civil war, Hobbes believed it was the king who had kept order and the rebelliousness of the people that had brought disaster.

The title of Locke's second treatise states that the purpose of the work is to understand the "True Original [origins], Extent, and End of Civil Government." Locke's core ideas concerning the origins of the state, the need to limit the monarch's* power, the need to equate authority with law, and the importance of protecting political and property rights* all reflect these concerns.[3]

This was no direct counterargument to Hobbes, who agreed both that for power to be legitimate it must serve the people, and that the people should be free to act in any way not forbidden by the law.

The two differed, almost exclusively, on practical matters. Hobbes saw the state of nature* as a violent place where life would be "solitary, poor, nasty, brutish and short."[4] The "leviathan" in Hobbes's work was the king, who protected the people both from each other and from themselves. For him, humanity sold its natural rights to the king in return for his protection.

Academic Influences

In assessing John Locke's *Two Treatises of Government*, it is impossible to disentangle its message from the influences of his particular group of close friends and colleagues.

Locke's education and his religious and family background saw him look for a theory of the state derived from nature and from society.[5] His proposals were a serious challenge to those who wanted to legitimize the power of a king or a parliament on religious grounds. Locke's affiliations with Oxford University, and his friendship with the likes of the Earl of Shaftesbury* and the statesman Lord John Somers,* allowed him to exchange radical ideas.

Locke was born in a time of change. The ideas of the ancient Greek philosopher Plato* had dominated European thought for more than two thousand years. But men like the philosopher René Descartes,* a contemporary of Locke's, had begun to challenge and modify this type of classical thought. In this light, Locke's ideas can be seen as an evolution of Hobbes's, inspired both by the events and by the spirit of the age.

The rational spirit of the Enlightenment was highlighting new ideas and inspiring people to question long-established ways of doing things. Locke may well have been arguing for a contemporary form of government in which the nation was governed by a monarch with limited powers, as some of his friends in the government desired. But his ideas were to have long-lasting effects well outside the politics of seventeenth-century England.

NOTES

1   See Richard Ashcraft, "Locke's Political Philosophy," in *The Cambridge Companion to Locke*, edited by V.C. Chappell (Cambridge: Cambridge University Press, 1994), 226–28.

2   See Robert Filmer, *Patriarcha and Other Writings*, ed. Johann Sommerville (London: Cambridge University Press, 1991).

3   Chappell, *The Cambridge Companion to Locke*, 228–30.

4   Thomas Hobbes, *Leviathan* (Ware: Wordsworth Editions, 2014), 97.

5   Peter Laslett, introduction to John Locke, *Two Treatises of Government*, ed. Peter Laslett, 2nd ed. (Cambridge: Cambridge University Press, 1988), 18–22, 40–45.

MODULE 3
THE PROBLEM

KEY POINTS

- At the time *Two Treatises* was written, thinkers were beginning to ask questions about how society should be governed.

- According to the dominant position, explained in different ways by other political theorists, kings obtained their right to rule from God.

- Locke's thinking continued a process that had begun with Thomas Hobbes,* defining the conditions of the contract that society entered into with its leaders.

Core Question

John Locke's *Two Treatises of Government* has an explicit overarching goal, and it could be argued that the aims of the second part, stated in the subtitle, represent this goal best. He wanted to discuss the "True Original [origins], Extent, and End of Civil Government," and he wanted to achieve this by understanding the nature of "political power."[1]

This question of where political power begins and ends, and what it is for, was both the central question in this work and the pivotal question of the time. Indeed, it is arguably one of the fundamental questions in all political thought. The fact that this was the key question of the day helps us understand why Locke was asking the question in the first place.

Disagreement on these matters had led to civil and social conflict throughout Locke's life, so, on a practical level, these questions meant the difference between stability and peace, uncertainty and war. On a

> ❝ By this breach of trust they forfeit the power the people had put into their hands, for quite contrary ends, and it devolves to the people. ❞
>
> John Locke, *Two Treatises of Government*

larger level, Locke was aware that these issues were not unique to England in the seventeenth century. So rather than simply writing for his own society, he chose to use philosophical reasoning, which potentially gives his work universal appeal.

The Participants

The political environment at the time *Two Treatises* was written provoked a debate that reached well beyond arenas of academic or political discussion. Most of these ideas could be split along rational lines of division, such as between Roman Catholics* and Protestants,* or else between those who favored the power of the king and those who favored the power of parliament.*[2]

As we have seen, the two most influential arguments that ran counter to Locke's view both arrived at the conclusion that the country should be governed by a monarch—but for different reasons.

Robert Filmer's* arguments were biblical in nature. Indeed, his line of thought cannot be properly understood outside a biblical context. God gave to the first man, Adam, complete control over his descendants, Filmer theorized. This political power was passed down from father to son through a system known as patriarchy.* Although no unbroken line could be traced, the line was, in Filmer's view, divinely preserved. Only a king could make laws, which meant, by definition, that the king was above all laws.

Thomas Hobbes's* view was far more grounded in reality than Filmer's. For Hobbes, spirituality was not the main issue when it came to government. He was more concerned with the practical necessities of good government. For Hobbes, nature was an unpleasant place to be, and though he borrowed the concept from a prior thinker, the Dutch philosopher Hugo Grotius,* he made colossal use of the analogy to formulate his theory of a social contract.*

The king received power not through God, but through a society that volunteered to abandon liberty in return for protection. The Hobbesian sovereign must therefore be all-powerful, controlling all aspects of society, so as to avoid a state of anarchy* with no government or law where the strong would prey on the weak.

Locke rejects this pessimism about human nature, believing that people can create societies that allow for toleration of differences, encourage material prosperity, and protect individual liberties.[3]

The Contemporary Debate

Political thought moved at a slower pace in the seventeenth century. Locke's views should be seen as a process that began with Hobbes (although, as we have seen, Hobbes also owed some debt to the ideas of Grotius).

Since the first treatise was a direct attack on the ideas put forward by Filmer, this should be seen as an implicit part of the debate. Locke disagrees utterly with Filmer. With Hobbes, on the other hand, Locke is modifying the theory of the social contract to an extent where a different conclusion is reached. Locke's views were, however, not formulated in isolation. Several other writers dealt with many of the same topics and even came to similar conclusions. His friend the political writer James Tyrrell,* for example, wrote a work called *Patriarcha non Monarcha*, which was initially far more influential in contradicting Robert Filmer's* arguments for absolute monarchy.* An even more radical text came from the republican* Algernon Sidney,* whose *Discourses Concerning Government* also went against Filmer.[4]

Although his work derives many of its ideas from other thinkers,

Locke combines his theories of property, social evolution, and political accountability in ways that create a cohesive theory of political rights based on universal principles and serve in some ways to justify revolution.* Locke's state of nature,* for instance, expands on Hobbes's ideas of instability and risk to property to argue that the protection of this property actually forms the basis of the social contract between people and their state.

Locke's influence stretched well beyond the seventeenth century. His views became an integral part of the political discourse that included thinkers such as Jean-Jacques Rousseau* and Thomas Paine,* who advocated complete political equality for citizens and who opposed monarchy in favor of rule by fellow citizens subject to the law and to free elections. Impressively, Locke's views have remained influential ever since.[5]

NOTES

1   John Locke, *Two Treatises of Government*, ed. Peter Laslett, 2nd ed. (Cambridge: Cambridge University Press, 1988), 267–68.

2   For a discussion of the immediate context of the work, see Peter Laslett, introduction to Locke, *Two Treatises*, 45–66.

3   For an interesting account of how Locke viewed colonialism as a means of creating ideal government, see Barbara Arneil, *John Locke and America: The Defense of English Colonialism* (Oxford: Oxford University Press, 1996).

4   Algernon Sidney, *Discourses Concerning Government* (London, 1698), accessed April 7, 2015, http://www.constitution.org/as/dcg_000.htm.

5   See Martyn P. Thompson, "The Reception of Locke's Two Treatises of Government 1690–1705," *Political Studies* 24, 2 (1976): 184–91; see also Ellis Sandoz, *A Government of Laws: Political Theory, Religion, and the American Founding*, vol. 1 (Columbia: University of Missouri Press, 2001).

THE AUTHOR'S CONTRIBUTION

KEY POINTS

- Locke rejects the idea that a king's power comes directly from God and that the king's subjects owe absolute obedience to him.
- His argument is based largely on the idea of a social contract,* where a social group agrees to be ruled in return for rights that are protected. Governments that do not provide such protected rights are not legitimate.
- Locke's work took existing ideas, but developed both new ideas and new conclusions out of them.

Author's Aims

In *Two Treatises of Government*, John Locke puts forward a number of central ideas and addresses them in a uniquely inventive way. Although he clearly draws on his practical experience of politics, he avoids any actual reference to English history or constitutional law—and this was somewhat unusual for the writing of the time.[1] Considering the political acts and thought of men like his patron and friend the First Earl of Shaftesbury,* who attempted to intervene in the succession to the throne of the United Kingdom, and in Locke's adaptation of Thomas Hobbes's* ideas, it is clear that Locke was working in response to the intellectual and political landscape of his day.

He arrives at his conclusions by first discussing his rejection of the idea that kings are divinely ordained to rule. In a manner consistent with his background as a physician, once he diagnoses the problems, he proceeds to offer improvements or corrections—cures, in other

> ❝ The power that every individual gave the society, when he entered into it, can never revert to the individuals again, as long as the society lasts, but will always remain in the community, because without this there can be no community, no common-wealth. ❞
>
> John Locke, *Two Treatises of Government*

words. Despite building on the ideas of men like the French political theorist Jean Bodin*—whose view of protecting property rights* as part of natural law* placed a genuine limit on the power of the sovereign[2]—Locke distinguishes his ideas by offering solutions with both universal and practical applications. If the text can be viewed as a challenge to orthodox thought, that is testament to the radical ideas it contains.

Although Locke's ideas are often seen as being in the tradition of political liberalism*—which emphasizes individual rights and responsibilities in government, and limits its powers—they are also highly community-minded. This emphasis on the rights of the individual was not commonplace in the seventeenth century. Ideas of democracy* had been refuted by the Greek philosopher Plato* more than two thousand years before, and the reverence which most— though not all—philosophers of this time felt towards classical thought guided, and perhaps even served to stagnate, political thought long after Locke's death.

Approach

Locke's use of language reflects the spirit in which he enters into what should be seen as the political debate of his age. His choice of the word "common-wealth," for example, does not simply suggest simply a different name for a state but, rather, a state genuinely concerned with the "common wealth," or well-being of all. Locke goes on to finish the text by stating that when this common wealth is ignored or abused, the people have the right to place a new government in power or even to create entirely new political institutions, "as they think good."[3] If Locke was not advocating democracy as it would be understood today, he was advocating a form of democracy based on individualism, a social contract between the citizen and the political class, and a concern for the common good. This places the work quite firmly in the tradition of liberal political thought.

In the same way, Locke's views that political states begin as a contract to protect property and evolve into systems where law is sovereign (has supreme power), even over the king or queen, was a unique addition to human thought. The execution of Charles I* in 1649, the restoration of the monarchy* under Charles II* in 1660, and the deposing of James II* in 1688 were all fresh memories in England at the time Locke wrote *Two Treatises* and each event marked the triumph of one side of the political spectrum over the other. Locke's views justify the removal of two kings and can be read in two ways—as a genuine call to revolution on the one hand, and as an argument that a monarch could be removed *only* if an abuse of power had occurred on the other.[4] In other words, Locke's arguments could be cited as justification for the major, tumultuous, events of seventeenth-century English history.

It is important to remember that while Locke does not refer to these historical events at all, the subtext would certainly have been understood by those reading the work. His most enduring and unique contribution is still the fact that the text paved the way for a justification of the political actions of the past, while at the same time advocating a new form of future government—strong, fixed-term, and subject to the will of the people.

Contribution In Context

In chapter 5 of the second treatise, Locke writes that there is "land enough in the world to suffice double the inhabitants had not the invention of money, and the tacit agreement of men to put a value on it, introduced (by consent) larger possessions."[5] This leads to his proposition that the invention of money allowed people to acquire more property than they could possibly use and, thus, led to scarcity that would not exist otherwise. In doing so Locke is engaging in a thought experiment, known as a state of nature,* which begins with us asking ourselves to imagine what life was like before the invention of society and the political institutions that belong to it.

Locke's second treatise should be viewed as a form of social contract theory that borrows heavily from Hobbes. But the two men differed significantly on one point. For Hobbes the state of nature was a violent, lawless place where the strong preyed on the weak. Locke, on the other hand, felt that the state of nature was governed by laws, and was not without reason. His contribution, then, was to expand the argument, taking existing ideas and developing new ideas and conclusions from them. Concepts such as the basic goodness of humanity, for example, were absent in Hobbes's argument.

Although such a realization led to the inevitable conclusion that the substance of Locke's work is inextricably linked to Hobbes by way of the social contract, two important caveats must be considered. First, Locke's first treatise is not a continuation of prior thought, but more the dismantling of it. Second, though he traveled the same path as Hobbes, Locke's conclusion is very different. Informed by the social contract, Locke's interpretation takes the reader off on a tangent that ultimately leads to a liberal state.

NOTES

1   For an excellent overview of Locke's career, see J.R. Milton, "Locke's Life and Times," in *The Cambridge Companion to Locke*, ed. V.C. Chappell (Cambridge: Cambridge University Press, 1994), 5–25.

2   For a more detailed list of those who influenced Locke, see Martyn P. Thompson, "The Reception of Locke's Two Treatises of Government, 1690–1705," *Political Studies* 24, 2 (1976): 184–85.

3   John Locke, *Two Treatises of Government*, ed. Peter Laslett, 2nd ed. (Cambridge: Cambridge University Press, 1988), 428.

4   For the view that Locke wants to incite rebellion, see Richard Ashcraft, "Locke's Political Philosophy," in *The Cambridge Companion to Locke*, ed. V.C. Chappell (Cambridge: Cambridge University Press, 1994), 226–51. Alternatively, for a view that Locke's motives are unclear, see John Dunn, *The Political Thought of John Locke: An Historical Account of the Argument of the "Two Treatises of Government"* (Cambridge: Cambridge University Press, 1982).

5   Peter Laslett, introduction to Locke, *Two Treatises*, 293.

SECTION 2
IDEAS

MAIN IDEAS

KEY POINTS

- Locke argues that although people give up certain rights in order to live in society, there is a limit to how much power they surrender.

- He theorizes about the origins of political power and tries to make sense of them.

- Locke's old-fashioned language is sometimes hard to follow, but the way he builds arguments logically helps modern readers keep pace with the work.

Key Themes

The main themes of John Locke's *Two Treatises of Government* are a discussion of the origins of political power, its role in organizing the institutions of the state, the limits of state power, and the conditions under which that power can be overthrown and replaced. Within these themes are several other major topics, including property rights,* slavery,* paternal power, and the division of political power.

The emergence of Locke's themes are best considered in two parts. In the first treatise, he follows the arguments of the political thinker Robert Filmer* concerning the absolute power of the monarch.* Filmer traced this power from the biblical account of Adam and his role as father of all humankind. Locke, in a manner reminiscent of Niccolò Machiavelli's* catalog of the various ways in which a ruler can come to power in his book *The Prince*,[1] examines, and then demolishes, all the different claims that Filmer makes for Adam's power and how these have filtered down to the English monarchy.

The second treatise takes up many of these same themes but does

> **"** No arts; no letters; no society and which is worst of all, continual fear and danger of violent death; and the life of man, solitary, poor, nasty, brutish, short. **"**
>
> Thomas Hobbes, *Leviathan*

so in an evolutionary manner, tracing political power from primitive society and the development of private property and money. It is an approach that allows the reader to fully understand Locke's assumptions about human nature, society, and the state, and what the state was ultimately for. Once these assumptions are defined and explained, he then describes how political institutions should be divided into a lawmaking power and a law-enforcing power, how the leadership of the state can be corrupted, and what society can do to correct abuses of power.

Exploring The Ideas

Since the main themes center on the question of power, it is possible to define the rights of man as one of the text's key features. Locke does not advocate a free society; instead he envisions a contract between the government and the people.

The first treatise and the second are separate arguments, even if the first supports the second.

In a society as deeply religious as that of seventeenth-century England, Locke's readers would have had to wrestle with the problem of a divinely appointed monarch: if the power of the king came from God, then any limit placed upon that would be in opposition to God's will, a belief known as "absolutism."*

Locke rejects that notion by ridiculing Filmer's belief that a ruler inherits his position from the first man of the Bible, Adam. Locke denies that Adam had been granted any power over his descendants and argues the practical impossibility of tracing proper heirs through history.

Such an observation might well seem superfluous in less religious times. But for Locke's contemporaries it provided the freedom required to consider the specific conditions needed to *entitle* a government. It also allowed for a discussion of the limits of legitimacy, specifically with regard to when it is permissible to change the leadership and the institutions of the state.

This rejection of absolutism is followed by a hypothetical account of how society develops into a political state.

The Glorious Revolution of 1688,* which replaced the Catholic King James II* with the Protestant King William III* and his wife, Queen Mary II,* provided an important—yet deliberately omitted— backdrop to the main theme. If you thought that James had abused his power, then you could point to Locke for a justification of his removal. But you can also see that William and Mary, being subject to the laws of parliament* (as they were), fit within Locke's model of good statesmanship.[2]

The specific relevance of *Two Treatises* to the political events of the day should not, however, be allowed to detract from the central theme's universal appeal. The idea that governments serve to protect property rights, and that their power is granted by the people, leads to one overriding and logical conclusion: what the people give, the people can also take away.

The right to replace rulers when abuses occur remains one of the text's most influential ideas.

Language And Expression

Though Locke's writing can seem old-fashioned to modern readers, he builds on his ideas in a logical and concise way. It should, however, be noted that Locke's first treatise is less accessible. Its reference to Filmer and its detailed biblical analysis assumes a substantial amount of awareness of these other texts on the part of the reader.

Nevertheless, Locke's way of building a case gradually, making sure the parts support one another effectively, helps to offset the difficulties of trying to understand seventeenth-century English. The cohesiveness and comprehensiveness of his discussion have made this text applicable and inspirational to a variety of politicians, students of politics and law, and political theorists.

Locke's property-based analysis of political rights has been especially influential. By coining new concepts such as "commonwealth,"* he inspired the notion of a society where everyone has a stake in its prosperity. Such a powerful idea was more than a radical statement; it inspired debates and even found its place in documents such as the American Declaration of Independence,* which set out the grounds for the colonists'* rejection of British rule, largely along Lockean lines of violation of property rights and personal privacy.* The continuing dominance of the United States and its constitutional* ideas in world affairs has made this particular influence globally important.[3] Indeed, Locke is viewed as the father of liberalism*— even if he did not use the term in *Two Treatises*.

Locke's ideas were complete and logical, but necessarily rudimentary. He was describing an ideal form of government, not imposing rules and regulations on existing ones. It was not until the Declaration of Independence in 1776 and the successful conclusion of the War of Independence* of the young United States that these ideas were put into practice.

NOTES

1   Niccolò Machiavelli, *The Prince*, trans. George Bull (London: Penguin, 1987).

2   For a very interesting discussion of Locke's immediate aims for this work and the Glorious Revolution, see Lois G. Schwoerer, "Locke, Lockean Ideas, and the Glorious Revolution," *Journal of the History of Ideas* 51, 4 (1990): 531–48.

3   For further discussion on American law and Locke, including its international ramifications, see Ellis Sandoz, *A Government of Laws: Political Theory, Religion, and the American Founding*, vol. 1 (Columbia: University of Missouri Press, 2001).

SECONDARY IDEAS

KEY POINTS

- Locke emphasizes the themes of colonialism* and slavery.*
- The work references the American colonies* with regard to property. Locke argues that Europeans could make better use of the land than the Native American* population.
- Locke's investigation of divine legitimacy and the passing of property and titles to the firstborn son on death could still be relevant today.

Other Ideas

The most important secondary themes in John Locke's *Two Treatises of Government* are colonialism and slavery, which should be placed in relation to Locke's wider argument.

The related discussions of slavery are meant to demonstrate the dangers of the theory of God-given authority—divine right,* or "absolutism."* Locke's belief is that "a man, not having the power of his own life, cannot, by compact, or his own consent, enslave himself to any one, nor put himself under the absolute, arbitrary power of another, to take away his life, when he please."[1]

Here Locke is laying down the groundwork of natural rights,* ideas that would ultimately end slavery as a political institution. As with many of Locke's ideas, he is describing an ideal state. It would take years before it would become a reality.

References to America and its native inhabitants are also linked to Locke's belief that political society is initially created by the need to protect property. He uses this example to prove that his hypothetical

> ** " ** Nobody can give more power than he has himself;
> and he that cannot take away his own life, cannot give
> another power over it. **" **
>
> John Locke, *Two Treatises of Government*

ideas about the development of society have some basis in reality. But he also uses it to show that England had a legitimate right to colonize because its utilization of property was more efficient and so more useful to the common good than that of the Native Americans.[2] Unlike Locke's dismissal of patriarchy,* with its reliance on frequent biblical references, his discussion of colonialism is vivid and easy to read. By first demonstrating that people gain a right to property by adding labor to it, he is then able to argue that colonial expansion was a means of adding labor and value to land that was underused, so was therefore a legitimate enterprise.[3]

Exploring The Ideas

In addition to making a case that political power should be limited and based on the common good, Locke's secondary themes can be useful in making a case for interventions in another state's affairs if it can be justified to be in the common interest.

For Locke, property rights were untouchable. So the question of ownership was pressing. While such ideas are central to the work's principal themes, they develop special significance when applied to the specific concerns of the American colonies. The taking of land from indigenous people required no small degree of justification since property, in Locke's view, was sacrosanct.

Students and academics interested in questions of colonial domination and its relation to liberal* political thought, which seem contradictory at first glance, have also used Locke's defense of colonialism and his descriptions of America as keys to understanding this paradox.[4]

While the text is discussed for what it says about individual political and property rights, it can also be important for those who question the very basis of power relationships in society between men and women, and the proper role of states intervening in the affairs of another state.

Slavery is another important theme. In Locke's thorough and systematic rejection of patriarchy in the first treatise, he demonstrates that the Bible itself can be used to justify individual rights and political equality.[5] These ideas seem to flow naturally into questions surrounding the idea of slavery, where Locke feels it is necessary to emphasize the limits of any single person's power.

Overlooked

Though *Two Treatises* is one of Locke's most cited works, overall, and is generally considered to be a foundational text in liberalism and modern political thinking on universal human rights,*[6] the second of the treatises has received the most attention.

Having traditionally attracted little interest, the first treatise is rarely referred to in other major political works. And what little interest there was in Locke's argument against patriarchal monarchy,* and against unconditional political obedience, has naturally ebbed away with time.

His argument about the difficulty of establishing divine legitimacy* on any rational grounds and the potential for abuse of a state's citizens is harder to understand from a modern perspective, where liberal democracies are prominent in world politics. Nevertheless, the ideas of the first treatise have not become irrelevant over time. Such ideas could even have major implications for understanding the effects of present-day authoritarian* regimes.

Thinkers like the historian Herbert Rowen* suggest that the first treatise is neglected in scholarly literature in part due to a lack of appreciation of its dual role.[7] The work is not simply a rejection of Robert Filmer's* theory on the divine right of monarchs. It is also a statement of Locke's own belief that power based on primogeniture* (the passing of property and titles to the firstborn son, or the closest male heir) is fundamentally wrong.[8] In effect, it diagnoses the disease of political thought for which his second treatise offers a cure.

The fact that the first portion of the text, with its detailed use of passages from the Bible, is largely neglected also reflects a long period in which religious considerations were not taken seriously in assessing political values. However, even Western political theorists have begun to consider in a more detailed manner the role of religious belief in forming political ideas. In a similar vein, scholars such as the political scientist Barbara Arneil* have argued that Locke's specific references to America and its native population have been either ignored or misinterpreted. These passages (primarily found in chapter 5) are seen as especially ripe for reinterpreting the historical role of the work in legitimizing both colonial rule and the expansion of capitalism.*[9]

Human rights theorists such as the scholar David Held,* who struggle to balance advocacy for universal human rights with local customs and morality, have also taken up this type of critique. The trend towards political and economic globalization* has made resolving this tension even more urgent than it was in Locke's time. Why? Because most states are now subject to a variety of international laws requiring them to respect certain human rights internally and to intervene to protect these rights when they are fundamentally threatened in another state.[10]

NOTES

1 John Locke, *Two Treatises of Government*, ed. Peter Laslett, 2nd ed. (Cambridge: Cambridge University Press, 1988), 284.

2 Barbara Arneil, *John Locke and America: The Defence of English Colonialism* (Oxford: Oxford University Press, 1996), 1–2.

3 Locke, *Two Treatises*, 290–302. See also Arneil, *John Locke and America*.

4 Barbara Arneil, "The Wild Indian's Venison: Locke's Theory of Property and English Colonialism in America," *Political Studies* 44, 1 (1996): 60–74.

5   Locke, *Two Treatises*, 171–95.

6   For example, Michael E. Goodhart, "Origins and Universality in the Human Rights Debates: Cultural Essentialism and the Challenge of Globalization," *Human Rights Quarterly* 25, 4 (2003): 935–64.

7   See Herbert H. Rowen, "A Second Thought on Locke's First Treatise," *Journal of the History of Ideas* 17, 1 (1956): 130–32.

8   Rowen, "A Second Thought," 130–32.

9   See Arneil, *John Locke and America*.

10 See Goodhart, "Origins and Universality."

MODULE 7
ACHIEVEMENT

KEY POINTS

- Locke's ideas were seen as very important by later generations. US statesman Thomas Jefferson,* who was the principle author of the Declaration of Independence, named him one of the three most important modern thinkers.

- The American War of Independence* helped give weight to Locke's views about accountable government.

- Some religious thinkers have criticized the book because, by over-highlighting individual rights, it doesn't pay enough attention to a person's duties towards others.

Assessing The Argument

Although John Locke's *Two Treatises of Government* largely reflects the political and philosophical concerns of his time in late seventeenth-century England, it is generally seen as more significant and relevant to political debate now than it was at the time of its publication. In part, this is because the text was discovered and championed by prominent eighteenth-century thinkers such as the philosopher David Hume,* who said that it captured the very essence of the political ideas of its time, and the statesman Thomas Jefferson, who named Locke one of the three most important modern thinkers.[1]

It is possible that not even Locke realized the full potential of his arguments. His work helped explain the tense political climate of 1688 as William of Orange ascended to the throne of the United Kingdom as William III* after the Glorious Revolution.* Indeed, at the time of its publication in 1689, the English Parliament* had already managed

> 66 We hold these truths to be self-evident, that all
> men are created equal, that they are endowed by their
> Creator with certain unalienable Rights, that among
> these are Life, Liberty and the pursuit of Happiness. 99
>
> The US Declaration of Independence

to limit the king's powers. So in some ways Locke was describing a system of government that already existed. Though earlier drafts of *Two Treatises* pre-date the creation of a limited monarchy,* the publishing date corresponds with its existence as a political reality. In this sense, it is clear that Locke set out to justify this new political arrangement.

The will of the people, however, was not truly reflected in this new system. In fact, the vast majority of people had not been granted a say in the running of affairs. Many powers were still invested only in the king, and true democracy* would not arrive in England until many years later. So it is important to understand that Locke was not advocating a democratic society, even if democratic principles can be seen as the logical end point of Locke's social contract.* It took later thinkers like Jean-Jacques Rousseau* to highlight the need for more general participation in government.

Achievement In Context

Major intellectuals of the Enlightenment* like Hume, Thomas Jefferson, and the political philosopher Charles Montesquieu* all used Locke's *Two Treatises* in various ways. Hume was attracted to Locke's attempts to explain the different categories of knowledge and his nonreligious account of natural law.* He also valued the fact that Locke's work reflected the full political thought of those English politicians who favored a monarchy that was also accountable to parliament.[2] Indeed, ever since the American War of Independence* against British rule in the 1770s, Locke's work has been seen as an authoritative statement of the principles of accountable government that derives from, and is answerable to, the people. With liberalism* dominant in international law after the end of World War II,* Locke's ideas about the legitimacy of the state, intervention, and when rebellion is justified have become even more relevant.

In Locke's time, no one could have predicted that states would bind themselves to international laws, such as the Responsibility to Protect* doctrine of the United Nations,* which requires those who have signed up to it to intervene in states where people's human rights are being fundamentally violated and their lives (or way of life) threatened.

Although the second treatise was written in part to justify colonialism* and European domination,[3] its ideas (especially in chapters 5 and 19) can now be used to explain why states may interfere in the affairs of another sovereign* state when the common good of its citizens is under genuine threat. The rejection of patriarchal* power as a legitimate basis for political power, as seen in the first treatise, has also become an important source of influence for modern feminists.*

Locke is considered a foundational political theorist in the United States. Lockean ideas are often invoked in contemporary political debates there, whenever people suspect that government is growing too powerful or exceeding its proper role in society. This could include objections to new forms of taxation, which are represented by right-wing opponents as theft of private property, as well as advocacy for stronger protections of speech and privacy rights.*

Limitations

Locke's *Two Treatises of Government* is a text that can be reinterpreted in different political and temporal contexts. Whether a king rules because God wills it, and whether he is due unconditional obedience, are not really burning political issues now. But Locke's beliefs that a government must be accountable and that people have the right to rebel under tyranny have seeped into our popular consciousness so much that they are now taken as political truths in liberal states.

Non-Western, non-Christian readers may struggle with the first part of the text. But the rest of *Two Treatises* has inspired resistance movements calling for individual freedoms and political accountability in many different political contexts, from the civil rights* movement in the United States to the rapid process of decolonization* from the 1940s onwards. Where early readers would have seen the discussion of America in the second treatise as justifying colonial domination for the good of the natives, those same natives now cite Lockean ideals of justice based on respect for property and the good of the community.[4]

This reassessment of Locke's liberal reputation is consistent with reactions to the book from the time of its publication onwards. It has always been seen as potentially powerful in its setting out of individual political rights, and yet it seems to contradict itself in its arguments for subjugation and its lack of a consistent source for universal natural law.* The more communitarian* ethos of some non-Western cultures (that is, the understanding that the community comes before the individual) has also led to Locke's work being seen as perhaps putting too much emphasis on individual rights and not enough on political duties. In fact, this critique is also seen in the Western tradition, particularly amongst religiously minded thinkers, who view this individualism as ignoring a person's duty to their fellow human beings.[5]

Despite these limitations, *Two Treatises of Government* may be considered foundational to present-day liberal political thought on sovereignty. It supports the views that sovereignty is derived from the people, and that the right to redress political abuses likewise remains with the people.[6]

NOTES

1   See David Hume, *An Enquiry Concerning Human Understanding: A Critical Edition*, vol. 3 (Oxford: Oxford University Press, 2000), xxxi, 149; see also Peter Laslett, introduction to John Locke, *Two Treatises of Government*, ed. Peter Laslett, 2nd ed. (Cambridge: Cambridge University Press, 1988), 14–15.

2   Martyn P. Thompson, "The Reception of Locke's Two Treatises of Government 1690–1705," *Political Studies* 24, 2 (1976): 184.

3   See Barbara Arneil, "The Wild Indian's Venison: Locke's Theory of Property and English Colonialism in America," *Political Studies* 44, 1 (1996): 60–74.

4   See Arneil, "The Wild Indian's Venison," 60–74.

5   Laslett, introduction to *Two Treatises*, 121–22.

6   See Laslett, introduction to *Two Treatises*, 122. Also Ellis Sandoz, *A Government of Laws: Political Theory, Religion, and the American Founding*, vol. 1 (Columbia: University of Missouri Press, 2001).

MODULE 8
PLACE IN THE AUTHOR'S WORK

KEY POINTS

- John Locke wrote *Two Treatises* toward the end of his life, so it was his last word on political philosophy.

- Locke wrote about many different subjects, but all his works were linked by his desire to encourage public stability and harmony.

- Locke's ideas in *Two Treatises* were profoundly influential in shaping the world's future political events. This makes it his masterpiece.

Positioning

John Locke was well into middle age before he wrote his *Two Treatises of Government*. Considering its attack on Robert Filmer's* *Patriarcha*, the first part of the work could not possibly have been begun before *Patriarcha* was published in 1679, and probably not before Locke purchased his own copy the following year.[1] Locke scholars such as Peter Laslett* argue that the two portions of the text were written during roughly the same period in Locke's life, from 1679 to 1683, meaning that he was between 47 and 51 years old.

The text reflects Locke's life experience and the political struggles he both lived through and participated in. This sense that it is a theory of government thoroughly grounded in reality and practicality is what makes it one of his most important works, alongside *An Essay Concerning Toleration* (1667–83) and *An Essay Concerning Human Understanding* (1689).[2]

Certainly, Locke was aware of Thomas Hobbes's* central argument in his book *Leviathan*, which did not justify the power of kings by

> **"** Property I have nowhere found more clearly explained,
> than in a book entitled, *Two Treatises of Government.* **"**
> John Locke, letter to Rev. Richard King, quoted in *Works*

looking to the Bible, as Filmer had done.

Whatever the truth of the matter, Locke's association with men like the Earl of Shaftesbury* marked him out for a long time as someone who had held strong beliefs on the role of monarchy* in society.

Two Treatises of Government could be considered Locke's last word on practical political philosophy. Although he did not publicly acknowledge the work as his, there is no evidence that he ever reconsidered his views in his final years.

Integration

Locke's other works were an eclectic mix of ideas sometimes far removed from the political subject matter he is most famous for. In his text *An Essay Concerning Human Understanding*, for instance, he was more concerned with the workings of the human mind, how simple ideas could be transformed into complex ones, and discrediting the idea that some knowledge was inborn.

Despite such tangents, Locke's body of work is coherent because it centers on his encouragement of political stability and public harmony. Even so, the subject matter of his work covers a vast range of topics, including medicine, religious orthodoxy and the state, the case for religious toleration, and natural philosophy.[3]

Locke's influence took some time to build. There is not much evidence that his *Two Treatises* were widely read until well after his death in 1704.[4] However, they became a major source of inspiration for the political thinking of some of the founders of both the American and French republics,* particularly his view that governments should be under a sovereign law* rather than a sovereign individual. This has given the work global implications.[5]

Despite its limited circulation, Locke's work was mentioned within his lifetime. The politician–philosopher William Molyneux* mentioned Locke's work as an important argument against absolute monarchy,* suggesting that Locke achieved his initial aim of making a strong case for his views. Walter Moyle,* a contemporary essayist, also acknowledged Locke's work, saying he had written what could be considered the "A. B. C. of politicks."[6]

Significance

The agreed view is that *Two Treatises* manages both to be very much of its time and yet to offer an account of politics that is general enough to be applied to a variety of political and historical contexts. Political thinkers from the 1700s to the present constantly refer to Locke's ideas, including those who were instrumental in important events like the American and French revolutions,* which helped to establish modern democratic* government.[7] Since he did not admit to having written *Two Treatises* when it was first published in 1689, the book clearly never made John Locke famous. Yet he had established his reputation long before as a man of learning and as a personal physician to important men like the Earl of Shaftesbury.

So Locke's authority really lies in his foresight with regard to how future political events would unfold. The American War of Independence* was fought between 1775 and 1783 in part over Locke's ideas about a government that was responsible to the people. And this war of ideas also inspired a revolution in France in 1789.* Locke's ideas would be enshrined in the 1788 US Constitution,* one of the world's most influential political documents. This makes *Two Treatises* one of the most influential political texts of all time. Locke also inspired many important political philosophers who came after him, including Thomas Paine,* Jean-Jacques Rousseau,* and Immanuel Kant.*

Not only is *Two Treatises* Locke's most important work, it is also one of the most important works in the entire canon of Western political philosophy. Once established, liberalism* as a philosophy proved to be an almost unstoppable force, leading to what the twentieth-century political theorist Francis Fukuyama* would describe as a "worldwide liberal revolution."[8]

NOTES

1   J.R. Milton, "Dating Locke's Second Treatise," *History of Political Thought* 16, 3 (1995): 356.

2   John Locke, *An Essay Concerning Toleration and Other Writings on Law and Politics, 1667–1683*, ed. J.R. Milton and Philip Milton (Oxford: Clarendon Press, 2006) and *An Essay Concerning Human Understanding*, ed. Kenneth P. Winkler (Indianapolis: Hackett, 1996). For an excellent overview of Locke's works and their relationship to his biography, see J.R. Milton, "Locke's Life and Times," in *The Cambridge Companion to Locke*, ed. V.C. Chappell (Cambridge: Cambridge University Press, 1994), 5–25.

3   For an interesting analysis of Locke on revolution in the second treatise, see Nathan Tarcov, "Locke's Second Treatise and 'the Best Fence against Rebellion'," *Review of Politics* 43, 2 (1981): 198–217.

4   Martyn P. Thompson, "The Reception of Locke's Two Treatises of Government 1690–1705," *Political Studies* 24, 2 (1976): 184.

5   See Ellis Sandoz, *A Government of Laws: Political Theory, Religion, and the American Founding*, vol. 1 (Columbia: University of Missouri Press, 2001).

6   Quoted in Laslett, introduction to *Two Treatises*, 5–6.

7   John Dunn, *The Political Thought of John Locke: An Historical Account of the Argument of the "Two Treatises of Government"* (Cambridge: Cambridge University Press, 1982), 6–10. These thinkers and revolutionaries include Voltaire, Jonathan Edwards, Thomas Jefferson, and many others.

8   Francis Fukuyama, "The End of History?", *National Interest* 16 (Summer 1989): 4.

8   Sawyer, *Seven Military Classics,* 149.

SECTION 3
IMPACT

MODULE 9
THE FIRST RESPONSES

KEY POINTS

- Locke never really acknowledged that he had written *Two Treatises*, and he made no clarifications to points he'd made that other thinkers struggled with.

- Locke's friend James Tyrrell* tried to push Locke to make *Two Treatises* more philosophically sound, without being altogether successful.

- The line that runs from Locke's thinking to modern liberal* states is still intact.

Criticism

John Locke was reluctant to acknowledge the fact that he had written *Two Treatises of Government*, and given the book's limited circulation— even by the standards of the day—there was little or no critical response to it during his lifetime.

Locke died in 1704, just five years after *Two Treatises* was published, so he did not have much time to respond to criticism, even if he had been of a mind to do so. The essayist Charles Leslie's* 1703 work *The New Association* rejected Locke's arguments outright.[1] Leslie argued that kings ruled by divine right,* and spent much of his career supporting King James II* and the established English church. There was also some private criticism of the work in letters from Locke's friend and fellow political thinker James Tyrrell. Serious engagement with Locke's work started much later, when thinkers such as David Hume* began analyzing *Two Treatises* as a statement of the principles of the Glorious Revolution* of 1688.

One of the main criticisms of the text has been Locke's

> **❝** The exercise of power beyond right is ... not for the good of those who are under it, but for his [the ruler's] own private separate advantage. **❞**
>
> John Locke, *Two Treatises of Government*

inconsistency as a philosopher. Tyrrell's correspondence with Locke shows that he wrote to him no less than six times after the work was published, asking him to expand on his definition of natural law.* This was seen as a crucial element that would allow a challenge to the ideas of Thomas Hobbes,* who was often derided as an atheist. Tyrrell was well aware that Locke's views on natural law incorporated the existence of God. But Locke seemed unable or unwilling to fully work out his views on this issue.[2]

Although Locke's reputation as a philosopher has been frequently criticized, his reputation as a political theorist was greatly aided by his linking of political and property rights.* It was further strengthened when his support for the Glorious Revolution's recognition of the supremacy of parliament* over the monarch* was proven to be a sustainable and successful model for governing.

Responses

Locke seems to have been very resistant to any criticism aimed at the work. As not many people knew Locke was the author, very few could respond to him directly. His friend James Tyrrell, however, was well aware of Locke's secret.

Tyrrell seemed to want to make *Two Treatises* more philosophically sound in order to find a better counterargument to the work of Thomas Hobbes. Hobbes had based his philosophical arguments both on biological determinism*—the idea that people do not have free will, and behave according to the demands of their bodies—and on mathematical principles. Tyrrell felt that Locke's inclusion of God in explaining what people commonly understood as good and evil was desirable, but that it was not strong enough to refute Hobbes's nonreligious views on the state of nature.*3

We know of six letters exchanged between Locke and Tyrrell in which Locke attempts to give a deeper explanation of his ideas. None satisfy Tyrrell. The most that Locke was willing to do was to criticize Hobbes's position that people were not bound to obey natural law* in the absence of the state. Otherwise, he told Tyrrell that he simply "declined the discourse."4 This raises the intriguing possibility either that he did not feel capable of debating with Hobbes directly, or that he was simply more concerned with creating useful theories of the state than he was with creating coherent philosophical theories.

Conflict And Consensus

Locke's unwillingness to listen to or engage with criticism meant there was no real change in his positions. There was no possibility of satisfying the desires of sympathetic readers like Tyrrell for a more rigorous philosophy, nor of answering critics who actually disagreed with him.5 It may be that Locke considered that his other works spoke for themselves. Alternatively, he may have been so concerned about acknowledging that he wrote *Two Treatises* that he thought it was too dangerous to get involved in major debate.

Whatever the case, just as Tyrrell felt that some of Locke's ideas needed developing, later thinkers also wanted to take Locke's ideas to another level. But the line that runs from Locke to modern liberal states is intact. His idea of a social contract* between governments and the people they serve is timeless. Only the details of the contract needed to be altered to fit specific situations. When the American colonies* objected to British rule during the American colonial crises, for example, Locke's idea that people should rebel against a bad government collided with this new political reality.

Locke should be seen as offering the intellectual underpinnings of liberalism. The logical conclusions drawn from these ideas and their implementation were left to other people in other times.

NOTES

1   Charles Leslie, *The New Association* (Gale ECCO, Print Editions, 2010).

2   Peter Laslett, introduction to John Locke, *Two Treatises of Government*, ed. Peter Laslett, 2nd ed. (Cambridge: Cambridge University Press, 1988), 79–82.

3   Laslett, introduction, 79–82.

4   Laslett, introduction, 80.

5   Locke's primary engagement with his critics was in defense of his *Essay on Human Understanding*, of which he acknowledged authorship.

THE EVOLVING DEBATE

KEY POINTS

- *Two Treatises of Government* has been an inspiration to people struggling against tyranny, demanding civil rights,* and striving for political independence.

- Political thinkers of all kinds have been influenced by Locke, from political economists to Marxists.* But it is liberals* who have drawn the most from him.

- Conservatives* who favor limited government and individual freedom would strongly relate to Locke.

Uses And Problems

John Locke's *Two Treatises of Government* has inspired those struggling for civil rights, political independence, and freedom from tyranny since the late eighteenth century. Political thinkers of many kinds have identified with the work's ideas. Locke influenced thinkers like the radical French writer Voltaire,* and the Genevan philosopher Jean-Jacques Rousseau,* as well as many of the founding fathers of the United States, including Thomas Jefferson.*

The term "Lockean" has even been created to describe people who subscribe to his way of thinking. Prominent Lockeans include the French political philosopher Charles Montesquieu,* who appreciated Locke's version of the state of nature* and his understanding that law was central to the character of the state.[1] Locke's argument that political power must be divided between a legislative* (lawmaking) and an executive* (law-enforcing) arm, with the former being the more important, was also highly influential.[2] This idea was particularly useful to the thinking of American statesman

> **❝** I should be pleased with the liberty which inspires the English genius if passion and party spirit did not corrupt all that is estimable in this precious liberty. **❞**
> Voltaire, *Candide*

James Madison,* who is often referred to as the "father" of the US Constitution.*

Long-term considerations of the text generally reduce its essential contributions to political thought to two points. First is the emphasis on the primary importance of government's legislative branch. Second is the connection Locke draws between economic and political issues in his description of how political society developed from earlier concepts of property, money, and the accumulation of wealth.

The first of these points has had global implications because of the importance of the explicitly Lockean elements of the US Constitution. This constitution enshrines the separation of power between those who create law and those who enforce it, as well as the requirement that the Constitution's laws should conform to its universalist principles. These principles were that the Constitution aimed to embody truths that applied universally—to all people.

The US Constitution also influenced the wording of several international documents, from the United Nations Charter* to the Universal Declaration of Human Rights.* This latter contribution is an essential part of the study of political economy and anticipated the way that it is common today for the success of a political regime to be gauged on its ability to generate wealth—preferably widespread wealth.

Schools Of Thought

Political thinkers of many kinds—past and present—identify strongly with the ideas in Locke's *Two Treatises of Government*.

Political economists, whose academic discipline did not exist in any proper sense at the time Locke wrote the work, have also applied his theory of property, money, and political obligation to an international regime of trade relationships, currency exchange, and dispute resolution that would have been difficult to imagine in the fiercely competitive imperial era in which Locke wrote.

Locke's focus on property rights* also drew the attention of Marxists, whose understanding of "ownership" is that which belongs to society as a whole.

However, it is to the political tradition of liberalism* that we must look to find Locke's true influence. Inspired by new challenges in resolving the tensions created by globalizing* economies and a renewed respect for local values, political philosophers have applied Locke's ideas of tolerance and development as a social good in their theories. The freedom of the individual is a fundamental part of many nations' identity—in liberal democracies, at least, where the need to rebel has been moderated by regular elections.

Although Locke's willingness to subjugate colonial* peoples for their own good is frowned upon, his advocacy for more efficient land use, and for the provision of food for the hungry and for communities to be provided with the means to be economically self-sufficient, have been commented on.[3] While some might argue that humanitarianism* is outside Locke's field of inquiry, his colonial administrative background places him comfortably within this discourse, albeit from a very different context.

In Current Scholarship

Prominent examples of more contemporary supporters of Locke's thought include the political philosopher John Rawls,* who is well known for his theories on how to create a more just social and political order, and the American political theorist Robert Nozick,* who advanced a libertarian* view of society based on Lockean values.

Although their ideas about the role the state should play in society are not the same, both appeal to Locke's ideas of personal freedoms, the common good, and tyranny—even if they come to very different conclusions about how they apply in the real world.

More recent self-proclaimed Lockeans include the constitutional* theorist Donald Lutz,* who specializes in accounts of how government should work on an institutional level, and has advised states on the formulation of new constitutions.

Most American conservatives would also strongly identify with Locke and his call for individual freedoms and limited government. This even extends to libertarians, who favor an extreme version of personal liberty in which government functions are limited to things such as defense and basic law enforcement.

All these thinkers have made use of those parts of the *Two Treatises* that best support their own positions. The comprehensive nature of the text and its conscientious use of rational philosophical, rather than historical, arguments makes its application to new problems quite flexible.

NOTES

1   Lee Ward, *John Locke and Modern Life* (Cambridge: Cambridge University Press, 2010), 140.

2   Ward, *John Locke and Modern Life*, 140.

3   For an example of interpretations of Locke in humanitarian discourse, see Michael E. Goodhart, "Origins and Universality in the Human Rights Debates: Cultural Essentialism and the Challenge of Globalization," *Human Rights Quarterly* 25, 4 (2003): 935–64.

MODULE 11
IMPACT AND INFLUENCE TODAY

KEY POINTS

- Locke's views that those who make laws and those who enforce laws should be separate entities are seen as an important protection against corruption.

- What sets Locke apart from many other political theorists is his belief that human beings are fundamentally decent.

- Many US political debates see those taking part draw on Locke's work to prove their arguments.

Position

It is worthwhile considering the postcolonial context in which John Locke's *Two Treatises of Government* is read today.

The work has informed recent debates on the question whether it is right to interfere in the affairs of another sovereign* state for humanitarian* reasons.[1] It has also played a role in economic debates about the relationship between economic globalization* and political independence.

Locke intended his ideas to have an economic—specifically capitalist*—resonance. This is revealed both by his professional history as a colonial administrator and by his discussion of colonial domination as a force for the common good in the fifth chapter of the second treatise.

Two Treatises helped to start the practice of emphasizing and specifying political rights more than political duties. Locke assumes that political society will require most citizens to do their duty instinctively for society to function, and he trusts the citizens to meet their obligations.

> **" Slavery is so vile and so miserable an estate in man ... that 'tis hardly to be conceived that an Englishman, much less a gentleman, should plead for it. "**
>
> John Locke, *Two Treatises of Government*

The political and governmental institutions of a state can easily move to repress political action and to structure opportunity so that wealth and status end up in the hands of a privileged few.[2] In this light, *Two Treatises* altered the balance of political discussion in favor of individual rights, establishing a tradition of linking political and economic development.

Its impact was both global and enduring and for this reason it is considered a cornerstone of liberal* thought.

Those in favor of humanitarian intervention and constitutional* governance also look to Locke's political values to justify their preferred political programs and actions. The universality of Locke's argument for property and political rights makes it an appealing argument for humanitarians who want to argue that states should (and sometimes must) intervene in the affairs of another sovereign state when that state's citizens are being threatened with genocide* or other violations of fundamental rights.[3]

This same universality, combined with Locke's separation of executive* and legislative* power, is appealing to liberal constitutional thinkers, who see this division as one of the best protections against the exercise of arbitrary power and against corruption.[4]

Interaction

Locke's political principles, as presented in *Two Treatises of Government*, are actively debated in academic, political, and judicial circles to this day.

As rulings tend to be based upon precedent (that is, what has happened in previous court cases), legal considerations are especially interesting.

One of the foremost nineteenth-century chief justices of the United States, John Marshall,* often made Locke's theory one of the central elements in his rulings. On matters of bankruptcy, he argued that, although contracts were made with an awareness that bankruptcy could occur, there was a more important assumption that people had the intention and presumption of honoring their commitments. Likewise, he used Locke's description of the state of nature* from the second chapter of the second treatise to outline exactly why the basis of civil law* is this presumption that people will perform their social and legal duties to one another in good faith.[5]

It is this same assumption of fundamental decency that Locke scholar Peter Laslett* notes in his assessment of what it is that sets Locke apart from other theorists of political rights and duties.[6]

This optimism about human nature in a political context must have had a powerful effect on a man like Marshall, who is generally considered to be a "strict constructionist"—or originalist*—in terms of his interpretation of the US constitution.*

The Continuing Debate

American constitutional debates are one of the most active areas for discussion of the meaning of Locke's work. Societies such as the John Locke Foundation* even name him the US's intellectual father, while his name is prominent in conservative* circles with regard to arguments favoring the expansion of capitalism and trade, a restricted scope for government action, and minimal taxation, as indicated in chapters 5, 7, and 9 of the second treatise.

On the other hand, liberal thinkers cite Locke for emphasizing the protection of minority rights, tolerance, and consideration of the common good, as discussed in both the introduction and the conclusion of the second treatise.

Politically motivated responses to Locke can be seen in major political parties or think tanks such as the Claremont Institute, which produces scholarly papers that support a conservative view of the US Constitution and law. There is overwhelming agreement that Locke is one of the most important theorists behind the actual text of the American Declaration of Independence* and the US Constitution. So those citing him do so out of a desire to persuade others of the legitimacy of their particular position on a particular political or legal issue.

Ideas of liberty are also constantly used in the field of international politics. Liberal democracies* often take the moral high ground when confronting totalitarian* regimes or societies where the freedom of the individual is not respected.

NOTES

1   Michael E. Goodhart, "Origins and Universality in the Human Rights Debates: Cultural Essentialism and the Challenge of Globalization," *Human Rights Quarterly* 25, 4 (2003): 963–64.

2   Peter Laslett, introduction to John Locke, *Two Treatises of Government*, ed. Peter Laslett, 2nd ed. (Cambridge: Cambridge University Press, 1988), 120–22.

3   For further discussion, see Goodhart, "Origins and Universality," 935–64.

4   For example, in Ellis Sandoz, *A Government of Laws: Political Theory, Religion, and the American Founding*, vol. 1 (Columbia: University of Missouri Press, 2001); also Donald S. Lutz, *The Origins of American Constitutionalism* (Baton Rouge: Louisiana State University Press, 1988).

5   R. Kent Newmyer, *John Marshall and the Heroic Age of the Supreme Court* (Baton Rouge: Louisiana State University Press, 2007), 261–63.

6   Laslett, introduction, 120–22.

WHERE NEXT?

KEY POINTS

- Locke's ideas were not explicitly linked to the political situation of his day. This has helped them remain relevant throughout history.

- The arguments in *Two Treatises*—especially where they touch on political and property rights*—still have universal appeal. They are not just limited to domestic politics.

- Locke's principles still offer good guidance on how to create a just and effective political order.

Potential

John Locke's effort to avoid linking his principles of state legitimacy and property to specific historical circumstances in his *Two Treatises of Government* has meant that the text continues to have a significant role in the discussion of these issues.

Locke's ideas have been developed in all kinds of interesting areas—to improve medical ethics, to make patent laws more socially responsible, and to ensure that labor is more justly compensated. This shows that the text may still find more social applications.[1]

The work may also be useful for finding principles of governance that are environmentally sound. Indeed, Locke's idea that legitimate political power is power that works to advance the common good has been considered a model for governance. His vision of America as a land of natural purity, for example, speaks for the social benefit of lands remaining common for the sake of the greater good.

In the same way, Locke's theory of labor could be significant in combating modern forms of slavery* and similar abuses.

> **"** Philosophers might be professionally interested in the philosophy of Locke, but everybody was interested in happiness, and everybody wrote about it. **"**
>
> Ian Davidson, *Voltaire: A Life*

Here, his idea that people own their own bodies and are entitled to the benefits of what they produce clearly goes against paying wages that do not sustain the basic needs of workers. The entire work has an underlying theme of rejecting oppression. As its opening lines state: "Slavery is so vile and so miserable an estate in man ... that 'tis hardly to be conceived that an Englishman, much less a gentleman, should plead for it."[2]

His second treatise further decries slavery as fundamentally unnatural. "Freedom from Absolute, Arbitrary Power is so necessary to, and closely joined with a Man's Preservation that he cannot part with it, but by what forfeits his Preservation and Life together."[3]

There are elements of the text that could be seen to have less relevance today—particularly the sections that justify colonialism.* It is no longer considered legitimate for a state to assert sovereign* authority over people who do not identify with it. Likewise, Locke's portrayal of the Native Americans* as not being entitled to land because they lacked the skills and will to develop it into agricultural or industrial sites makes for uncomfortable reading in an age where different societies are all considered equally valid. Ironically, this view is largely in accordance with Lockean ideas on social difference discussed in his *An Essay Concerning Toleration.*[4]

Despite these apparent difficulties, however, there is no sign that *Two Treatises of Government* is at any risk of losing influence as an integral part of Western political thought.

Future Directions

Current supporters of Locke's text include a wide variety of scholars of politics, philosophy, and economics, as well as politicians, judges, and the general public. They tend to be political liberals,* who stress individual rights and freedoms, economic freedom and noninterference from the government, and equality between people in terms of their rights and duties under the law.

Prominent examples include the political philosopher John Rawls,* who is known for his theories on how to create a more just social and political order, and Robert Nozick,* who advanced a libertarian* view of society based on Lockean values. Interestingly, both come to very different conclusions about how his ideas might be practically applied.

Indeed, Locke's arguments—especially where they touch on political and property rights—maintain an almost universal appeal that is not limited to domestic politics. The abuse of human rights* has been used as a pretext for more than one military intervention in recent history, and legitimate use of force to combat illegitimate abuse of power continues to be a strong motivating factor in how international relations play out.

The dominance of the Lockean form of the liberal state in international affairs, and in institutions such as the United Nations,* the World Trade Organization,* and the International Monetary Fund,* shows that his thinking is valued. It also means that this thinking still has impressive potential to influence political events via these institutions.

Summary

Two Treatises represents John Locke's most complete analysis of the origins, purposes, and limits of political and state power. It is one of a relatively small number of texts that are seen as foundational to liberalism, contemporary world affairs, and governance founded in a constitution.* It has been referred to in decisions made in the Supreme Court of the United States* and in major works of philosophy, and has been paraphrased in revolutionary statements and documents like the American Declaration of Independence.*

Although much of Locke's thought was derived, at least in part, from others or in response to others, he nonetheless formulated an original theory of the state by combining economic, political, theological, and even medical values into a cohesive whole.

The most important of these values is the idea that political power comes from the people and, more importantly, that it goes back to them when authorities abuse power and disregard the common good. The philosophical and hypothetical tone of his discussion has also made his ideas easy to apply to political and historical contexts other than his own. His insistence that political power, once established, can *only* remain legitimate when it is divided between the executive* (law-enforcing) and legislative*ˣ (lawmaking) branches and that it should be accountable to the people has been literally revolutionary. It was a major influence on eighteenth-century American and French radicals and on those who created the new constitutional orders following the revolutions* they successfully fought.

The influence of Locke's *Two Treatises* is likely to continue in the future. This text rejects patriarchy,ˣ locates the origin of political power in the people, champions the protection of political and property rights, and allows for the creation of new political orders when abuses have occurred. At its heart is the concern that citizens are treated as full social and political equals. As new social and political problems like the environment present themselves, Locke's principles of political power will continue to offer guidelines for considering how to create a just, effective, and free political order.

NOTES

1   For examples of these applications of Locke, see the following: Sigrid Sterckx, "Patents and Access to Drugs in Developing Countries: An Ethical Analysis," *Developing World Bioethics* 4, 1 (2004): 58–75; William Fisher, "Theories of Intellectual Property," in *New Essays in the Legal and Political Theory of Property*, ed. Stephen R. Munzer (Cambridge: Cambridge University Press, 2001), 168–200.

2   John Locke, *Two Treatises of Government*, ed. Peter Laslett, 2nd ed. (Cambridge: Cambridge University Press, 1988), 159.

3   Locke, *Two Treatises*, 302.

4   John Locke, *An Essay Concerning Toleration and Other Writings on Law and Politics, 1667–1683*, ed. J.R. Milton and Philip Milton (Oxford: Clarendon Press, 2006).

GLOSSARY

GLOSSARY OF TERMS

Absolutism (absolute monarchy): the belief that the government is legitimate on the basis that it exists and rules with God's implicit approval. So all subjects of the state owe the government unquestioned obedience.

American War of Independence: a conflict fought between 13 of Britain's North American colonies and the British Empire from 1775 to 1783, following the states' declaration that they were independent of British rule.

Anarchy: a belief in the creation of a political system or an actual state of being where nobody holds authority. Whilst originally the word was intended to convey lawlessness, Pierre Joseph Proudhon redefined it as a stateless society or societies where groups of individuals enter into voluntary agreements so far as the law is concerned.

Authoritarianism: a society that is best understood as involving submission to authority and the exercise of authority by a government.

Biological determinism: the argument that people act according to the needs and appetites of their bodies and so do not actually possess free will.

Capitalism: an economic theory that argues for private or corporate ownership of property and the use of property to create additional wealth or profit. Free markets, rather than governments, are what drive decision making in this system.

Catholic: a follower of the Roman Catholic Church, the largest and oldest of the Christian denominations. The head of the Catholic Church is the Pope, who resides in the Vatican in Italy. Approximately half of all Christians worldwide are Catholics.

Civil law: a system of law that deals with private matters between people in a society, as opposed to criminal or religious affairs.

Civil rights: rights based on citizenship in a political state. Civil rights generally protect the rights of individuals to express themselves freely and to participate fully in society.

Colonialism: the rule of the native population by people from another territory.

Colony: a country, occupied by settlers from another territory, that is under the control of those settlers.

Common-wealth: a term used by John Locke to describe the well-being of all in society.

Communitarianism: a way of thinking that values the good of a community over that of the individual.

Conservatism: a philosophy that generally seeks to maintain the existing political order and respect for tradition, and prefers political change to occur gradually rather than suddenly. It also emphasizes individual freedoms over social responsibilities.

Constitutionalism: a political theory that argues that every state should be run according to pre-established rules that apply equally to all citizens. Generally, it focuses on limiting state power in areas deemed to be private concerns in order to allow for personal liberty.

Declaration of Human Rights: a resolution passed by the United Nations in 1948 that obligates signatory states to protect individual rights to life and security, outlaws slavery and other abuses of individuals, and creates the universal right to political asylum and to freedom of expression, amongst a variety of other fundamental rights.

Declaration of Independence: ratified by the Second Continental Congress on July 4, 1776, this was a proclamation that Britain's 13 North American colonies no longer considered themselves to be part of the British Empire.

Decolonization: the process of being freed from colonial rule.

Democracy: a system of government in which the people exercise power, either directly or through elected representatives.

Divine right of kings: the notion that it was God who ultimately decided who would be king.

English Civil War: a war fought between the king and parliament between 1642 and 1651. It led to great political and social instability in England.

English liberties: derived from a long process in which the power of kings was limited in several important ways, the most significant of which was the inability to raise taxes. Tied into this framework were other traditionally English values, such as the right to be tried by a jury.

Enlightenment: also sometimes referred to as the Age of Reason, the Enlightenment began in Europe in the seventeenth and eighteenth centuries. Although tied to the Scientific Revolution, the Enlightenment did not constitute a single unified theory but was, rather, a general bias towards reason over superstition.

Exclusion crises: these began in 1679 and ended in 1681. The Exclusion Bill was a parliamentary attempt to stop the Protestant King Charles II's brother James from becoming the next king of England, Scotland, and Ireland. The bill was ultimately defeated and James took the throne as James II.

Executive: the part of government that is responsible for enforcing the law.

Feminism: a social theory that believes that men and women are socially and politically equal. It often, but not always, includes a critique of society as being male-dominated.

French Revolution (1789–99): a period of political and social upheaval that culminated in the execution of Louis XVI and the drafting of several transitory constitutions.

Genocide: the targeted destruction of a particular ethnic group.

Globalization: a process of international integration. Such integration takes many forms—economic, political, and cultural.

Glorious Revolution (1688): a name commonly given to the overthrow of English King James II by an alliance of parliamentarians and the Dutch ruler, William of Orange, who subsequently became William III of Great Britain and Ireland, ruling jointly with his wife, Mary II (daughter of James II). The reestablishment of the monarchy under William of Orange and Queen Mary was conditional on their accepting the authority of parliament in making law and marked a major evolution in English constitutional development.

Humanitarianism: a belief system holding that humanity should be completely concerned with the well-being of the human race.

Human rights: the basic rights and freedoms to which all people are entitled. These include life, liberty, and the pursuit of happiness, among others.

International Monetary Fund: the IMF was set up in 1944 and currently contains 188 nation members, all of which contribute to, and can borrow from, a collective pool.

John Locke Foundation: a US conservative think tank founded in North Carolina in 1990. The foundation is in favor of lowering taxes and decreasing spending on social welfare programs.

Legislature: the part of government that is responsible for making laws.

Liberal democracy: a political system that emphasizes human and civil rights, regular and free elections between competing political parties, and adherence to the rule of law.

Liberalism: a belief that government is created by society to promote the well-being of society. It also focuses on the rights of the individual person as a central concern.

Libertarianism: a political theory that argues that the state should be responsible for the defense of its populace and territory and for ensuring a very basic internal social order through policing and related functions. It otherwise advocates that the private market should be allowed to serve the rest of society's needs.

Marxism: the name given to the political system advocated by Karl Marx. It emphasizes an end to capitalism by taking control of the means of production from individuals and placing it in the hands of central government.

Monarchism: support for a system of government where a state is ruled by a person who is invested with royal authority. The monarch, as an institution, gives cohesion and legitimacy to all the other functions and organs of the state.

Native Americans: members of the numerous tribes and indigenous peoples living in North America at the time when European settlers arrived in the seventeenth century, prior to the formation of the United States of America. These peoples are sometimes referred to as indigenous Americans.

Natural law: the idea that human laws ultimately have their source in the way in which nature itself operates and that there are therefore certain timeless principles that are the foundation of all good laws.

Natural rights: a theory that asserts that all humanity possesses a number of rights that do not flow from any institution or law, but from nature itself. These rights are "inalienable," so cannot be denied.

Originalist (or strict constructionist): part of a legal school which argues that texts, in this case the United States Constitution, should be read and enforced in a way that is the closest possible to the original meaning and intent of those who wrote it.

Parliament: the lawmaking body in England, which consists of two houses: the House of Lords and the House of Commons. Today, it is the supreme political authority across the United Kingdom.

Patriarchal monarchy: a system of government that has a king at its head and where power is held and transferred through males only.

Patriarchy: the idea that power is rightly held by a senior male figure. Usually used in family contexts, this term also applies to states where males hold the power.

Primogeniture: the practice whereby property and hereditary titles are passed to the firstborn son or closest male heir in a family.

Privacy rights: the right of an individual to keep certain aspects of their life private. Such a concept is tied into notions of needing a warrant to search somebody's house.

Property rights: the laws created by governments regarding individual rights to own, sell, and benefit from property. Many economists believe that stable and firm property rights lead to economic stability and success.

Protestant: a follower of a Christian denomination that separated from the primacy of Roman Catholicism in the sixteenth century. Protestantism eventually rejected many of the rights and traditions of Catholicism and favored a more simplistic, less hierarchical structure.

Republicanism: a theory of the state that does not include a ruling monarch and generally claims that power originates from the people and that the ruler should remain accountable to them.

Responsibility to Protect: a doctrine that was ratified by the UN in 2006, stating that it is the responsibility of member states and the international community to protect people from genocide.

Revolution: in political terms, the overthrow of a government via non-legitimate means. The replacing of one administration with another during an election is not a revolution. Their removal by popular pressure, violent or otherwise, is a revolution.

Rye House Plot: this thwarted plan to assassinate King Charles II of England and his brother and heir James in 1683 led to a series of state trials of the supposed plotters.

Slavery: a system that allows human beings to be treated as property and therefore traded as a commodity.

Social contract: the idea that governments are formed when a social group agrees to be ruled by a ruler or ruling class so that their lives and certain fundamental rights can be protected. This idea implies that governments that do not provide these functions are illegitimate.

Sovereign law: a system where the law, rather than an individual such as a monarch, has supreme power.

Sovereignty: the right of any nation to govern itself without undue interference from outside sources.

State of nature: a philosophical tool that allows a thinker to imagine what human life was like before governments existed and so why people created government and what its proper purposes are.

Supreme Court of the United States: the final authority on legal interpretation in the United States. It has the power to decide whether laws are constitutional and to invalidate those that are not, as well as to rule on difficult cases and to establish legal precedents that are binding on lower courts.

Theological: relating to the study of religious beliefs or of God.

Totalitarianism: a political system in which the state exercises absolute or near-absolute control over society.

United Nations: an international organization founded in 1945 after World War II by 51 countries committed to maintaining international peace and security; developing friendly relations among nations; and promoting social progress, better living standards, and human rights. It now has 193 member states.

United Nations Charter: a charter that established the basic rules governing the United Nations and the relationship between its various members. It further describes certain international rights and obligations, violation of which can result in collective diplomatic, economic, and/or military intervention.

US Constitution: the supreme legal document of the United States. Ratified by all 13 states in 1790, it not only set out the type of government the country was to have, but also guaranteed each citizen certain rights and protections.

World Trade Organization (WTO): this deals with the global rules of trade between nations. Its main function is to ensure that trade flows as smoothly, predictably, and freely as possible.

World War II (1939–45): a global conflict that pitted the Axis Powers of Nazi Germany, Fascist Italy, and Imperial Japan against the Allied nations including Britain, the United States, and the USSR.

PEOPLE MENTIONED IN THE TEXT

Barbara Arneil is a professor of political science at the University of British Columbia. Her work is concerned with areas of identity politics and the history of political thought.

Jean Bodin (1530–96) was a French political thinker and legal scholar whose *Les six livres de la république* influenced theories of state sovereignty. He views sovereign rule as indivisible and absolute, but requires the ruler or rulers to be subject to certain natural laws, meaning that they must honor their commitments and must avoid taking private property without consent.

Charles I (1600–49) was king of England and Scotland from 1625 until his execution by parliamentarians at the conclusion of the English Civil War.

Charles II (1630–85) was king of England, Scotland and Ireland, defeated by Oliver Cromwell in 1651 and forced into exile. He returned to England in 1660 when the English Commonwealth ended and the monarchy was restored following Cromwell's death.

René Descartes (1596–1650) was a French philosopher who is considered the founder of modern philosophy. His book *Meditations on First Philosophy* is considered a cornerstone of all Western philosophical thought.

Robert Filmer (1588–1653) was an English political thinker whose major works include the book *Patriarcha* (1680), which argues that royal power is absolute. Consequently, he claims that in society all people are bound to obey and submit to the monarch.

Francis Fukuyama (b. 1952) is an American political scientist whose best-known work, *The End of History and the Last Man*, cites liberal democracy and free-market economics as the ultimate form of organizing society.

Hugo Grotius (1583–1645) was a Dutch philosopher who introduced the idea of natural, and therefore inalienable, rights of individuals. He was one of the first writers to lay the foundations of social contract theory.

David Held (b. 1951) is a professor of politics and international relations at Durham University. He argues for stronger international institutions and protections for human rights

Thomas Hobbes (1588–1679) was an English philosopher best remembered for his book *Leviathan*, in which he established what is now known as social contract theory. Hobbes championed government, specifically the monarchy, as the supreme defense against the chaotic "state of nature."

David Hume (1711–76) was a philosopher and key figure of the Scottish Enlightenment. His main ideas suggested that all things had a physical cause and should be discoverable via scientifically provable methods.

James II (1633–1701) was ruler of present-day Great Britain and Ireland from 1685 to 1688. He was suspected of being pro-French and pro-Catholic. He was deposed in favor of a limited, and explicitly Protestant, monarchy in the Glorious Revolution of 1688.

Thomas Jefferson (1743–1826) was the third president of the United States. As the principal author of the Declaration of

Independence he had a profound influence on the shaping of the nation and penned one of the best-known phrases in the English language, "all men are created equal."

Immanuel Kant (1724–1804) was a Prussian philosopher. His 1795 essay "Perpetual Peace" can be seen as a starting point of contemporary liberal thought.

Peter Laslett (1915–2001) was an academic at the University of Cambridge who studied the historical structure of the family and is also well known for his novel approaches to the works of Thomas Hobbes, John Locke, and Robert Filmer.

Charles Leslie (1650–1722) was an Irish cleric and controversialist who actively supported King James II and opposed the accession of William III and Mary II to the throne. He was well known for writing essays and books in support of the established Church of England and of divinely ordained monarchy.

Donald Lutz is a professor of political science at the University of Houston. His research focuses on American constitutional theory and, more recently, on constitutional theory in international contexts.

Niccolò Machiavelli (1469–1527) was an Italian diplomat, historian, philosopher, and political thinker, most famous for his book *The Prince*. In it, he suggests various ways in which a ruler can maintain power. It is often interpreted to suggest that "the ends justify the means" for rulers, meaning that any action that maintains power is acceptable, no matter how immoral.

James Madison (1751–1836) was the fourth president of the United States and one of the country's founding fathers. He helped draft the US Constitution and championed the Bill of Rights.

John Marshall (1755–1835) was chief justice of the US Supreme Court from 1801 to 1835. His opinions form the basis of much of present-day US jurisprudence, including the principle of judicial review, which means that laws can be declared unconstitutional and invalidated by the courts.

Mary II (1662–94) was the daughter of King James II. In 1688, parliament invited Mary and her husband William of Orange (later William III) to become joint king and queen, subject to the condition that they would be constrained by the will of parliament and the law.

William Molyneux (1656–98) was an Irish politician who formulated a philosophical question for Locke, called Molyneux's problem, which has continued to engage philosophers to the present day. He asked whether a blind man who was taught to recognize the shape of a cube and a sphere by touch would be able to distinguish it by sight, should he ever gain vision.

Montesquieu (Charles-Louis de Secondat, Baron de La Brède et de Montesquieu) (1689–1755) was a French aristocrat and one of the great political philosophers of the Enlightenment. His most famous book, *The Spirit of the Laws*, argues, amongst other things, that laws must naturally evolve from societies and must reflect the customs and values of those societies.

Walter Moyle (1672–1721) was a politician and historian who served in parliament as a supporter of increased trade and decreased clergy involvement in the state.

Robert Nozick (1938–2002) was an American political philosopher who taught at Harvard University. His books, such as *Anarchy, State, and Utopia* (1974), offered a libertarian alternative to John Rawls's system of thought. They emphasized individual rights and the absence of government intervention in society.

Thomas Paine (1737–1809) was a British political activist whose 1776 pamphlet *Common Sense* helped turn public opinion in America against British rule, leading to the American War of Independence. His *Rights of Man* (1791) was a defense of the French Revolution and of republican principles.

Plato (fourth century bce) was an ancient Greek philosopher. Founder of the Academy in Athens, the first university in the Western world, Plato, along with his teacher Socrates and his student Aristotle, laid the foundations of Western philosophy and science.

John Rawls (1921–2002) was an American moral and political philosopher who is most famous for his idea of the "Veil of Ignorance," which was first discussed in his book *A Theory of Justice* (1971). He proposed that, if we consider how we would structure society if we had no idea of our own position in it, we would be most likely to create a system that is as just as possible for those least well-off.

Jean-Jacques Rousseau (1712–78) was a Genevan philosopher and member of the Enlightenment movement whose writings heavily influenced the French Revolution. Both *Discourse on Inequality* and *The Social Contract* are cornerstones in modern political thought.

Herbert H. Rowen (1916–99) was an American historian of Dutch and early modern European history. He held a post at Rutgers University for 23 years until his retirement in 1987.

Anthony Ashley Cooper, First Earl of Shaftesbury (1621–83)
was an important English aristocrat and politician who held positions
under both the republican government of Oliver Cromwell and the
monarchy of Charles II. He was forced to flee into exile after
conspiring to have the future King James II excluded from the line of
succession because he was a Catholic.

Algernon Sidney (1623–83) was the son of Robert, Earl of
Leicester. He was a republican opposed to King Charles II and author
of *Discourses Concerning Government* (1698). He actively sought to
overthrow the king and was executed for treason.

John Somers, First Baron Somers (1651–1716) was an English
statesman who served in the government of King William III and
Queen Mary II. His notable positions include serving as attorney
general, lord high chancellor, and member of the Privy Council for
both Queen Anne and King George I. Among his achievements were
advocating the 1707 union of English and Scottish Parliaments and
ensuring that a Protestant claimed the British crown in 1714.

James Tyrrell (1642–1718) was an English political writer and a
close friend of John Locke. He rejected the idea of a divinely ordained
monarch and was well known for his *Patriarcha non monarcha* (1681),
which argued forcefully against Filmer.

Voltaire/François-Marie Arouet (1694–1778) was a French
Enlightenment writer who advocated, among other things, the rights
of the individual and the separation of church and state. His 1756 work
entitled *Essay on the Customs and the Spirit of the Nations* influenced the
way political thought looked at the past.

William III (1650–1702), also known as William of Orange, was a Dutch prince who was married to James II's daughter, Queen Mary II. In 1688, parliament invited William and Mary to become joint king and queen, subject to the condition that they would be constrained by the will of parliament and the law.

WORKS CITED

WORKS CITED

Armitage, David. "John Locke, Carolina, and the Two Treatises of Government." *Political Theory* 32, 5 (2004): 602–27.

Arneil, Barbara. *John Locke and America: The Defence of English Colonialism*. Oxford: Oxford University Press, 1996.

"The Wild Indian's Venison: Locke's Theory of Property and English Colonialism in America." *Political Studies* 44, 1 (1996): 60–74.

Ashcraft, Richard. "Locke's Political Philosophy." In *The Cambridge Companion to Locke*, edited by V.C. Chappell, 226–251. Cambridge: Cambridge University Press, 1994.

Chappell, V.C., ed. *The Cambridge Companion to Locke*. Cambridge: Cambridge University Press, 1994.

Davidson, Ian. *Voltaire: A Life*. 2nd ed. London: Profile Books, 2012.

Dunn, John. *The Political Thought of John Locke: An Historical Account of the Argument of the "Two Treatises of Government"*. Cambridge: Cambridge University Press, 1982.

Filmer, Robert. *Patriarcha and Other Writings*. Edited by Johann Sommerville. London: Cambridge University Press, 1991.

Fisher, William. "Theories of Intellectual Property." In *New Essays in the Legal and Political Theory of Property*, edited by Stephen R. Munzer, 168–201. Cambridge: Cambridge University Press, 2001.

Fukuyama, Francis. "The End of History?", *National Interest* 16 (Summer 1989): 4.

Goodhart, Michael E. "Origins and Universality in the Human Rights Debates: Cultural Essentialism and the Challenge of Globalization." *Human Rights Quarterly* 25, 4 (2003): 935–64.

Hobbes, Thomas. *Leviathan*. Ware: Wordsworth Editions, 2014.

Hume, David. *An Enquiry Concerning Human Understanding: A Critical Edition*. Vol. 3. Oxford: Oxford University Press, 2000.

Laslett, Peter. Introduction to John Locke, *Two Treatises of Government*, edited by Peter Laslett, 3–127. 2nd ed. Cambridge: Cambridge University Press, 1988.

Leslie, Charles. *The New Association*. Gale ECCO, Print Editions, 2010.

Locke, John. *An Essay Concerning Human Understanding*. Edited by Kenneth P. Winkler. Indianapolis: Hackett, 1996.

An Essay Concerning Toleration and Other Writings on Law and Politics, 1667–1683. Edited by J.R. Milton and Philip Milton. Oxford: Clarendon Press, 2006.

Two Treatises of Government. Edited by Peter Laslett. Cambridge: Cambridge University Press, 1988.

Lutz, Donald S. *The Origins of American Constitutionalism*. Baton Rouge: Louisiana State University Press, 1988.

Machiavelli, Niccolò. *The Prince*. Translated by George Bull. London: Penguin, 1987.

Milton, J.R. "Dating Locke's Second Treatise." *History of Political Thought* 16, 3 (1995): 356–90.

"Locke's Life and Times." In *The Cambridge Companion to Locke*, edited by V.C. Chappell, 5–25. Cambridge: Cambridge University Press, 1994.

Newmyer, R. Kent. *John Marshall and the Heroic Age of the Supreme Court*. Baton Rouge: Louisiana State University Press, 2007.

Rowen, Herbert H. "A Second Thought on Locke's First Treatise." *Journal of the History of Ideas* 17, 1 (1956): 130–32.

Sandoz, Ellis. *A Government of Laws: Political Theory, Religion, and the American Founding*. Vol. 1. Columbia: University of Missouri Press, 2001.

Schwoerer, Lois G. "Locke, Lockean Ideas, and the Glorious Revolution." *Journal of the History of Ideas* 51, 4 (1990): 531–48.

Sidney, Algernon. *Discourses Concerning Government*. London: 1698. Accessed April 7, 2015. http://www.constitution.org/as/dcg_000.htm.

Sterckx, Sigrid. "Patents and Access to Drugs in Developing Countries: An Ethical Analysis." *Developing World Bioethics* 4, 1 (2004): 58–75.

Tarcov, Nathan. "Locke's Second Treatise and 'the Best Fence against Rebellion'." *Review of Politics* 43, 2 (1981): 198–217.

Thompson, Martyn P. "The Reception of Locke's Two Treatises of Government 1690–1705." *Political Studies* 24, 2 (1976): 184–91.

Ward, Lee. *John Locke and Modern Life*. Cambridge: Cambridge University Press, 2010.

THE MACAT LIBRARY
BY DISCIPLINE

AFRICANA STUDIES

Chinua Achebe's *An Image of Africa: Racism in Conrad's Heart of Darkness*
W. E. B. Du Bois's *The Souls of Black Folk*
Zora Neale Huston's *Characteristics of Negro Expression*
Martin Luther King Jr's *Why We Can't Wait*
Toni Morrison's *Playing in the Dark: Whiteness in the American Literary Imagination*

ANTHROPOLOGY

Arjun Appadurai's *Modernity at Large: Cultural Dimensions of Globalisation*
Philippe Ariès's *Centuries of Childhood*
Franz Boas's *Race, Language and Culture*
Kim Chan & Renée Mauborgne's *Blue Ocean Strategy*
Jared Diamond's *Guns, Germs & Steel: the Fate of Human Societies*
Jared Diamond's *Collapse: How Societies Choose to Fail or Survive*
F. F. Evans-Pritchard's *Witchcraft, Oracles and Magic Among the Azande*
James Ferguson's *The Anti-Politics Machine*
Clifford Geertz's *The Interpretation of Cultures*
David Graeber's *Debt: the First 5000 Years*
Karen Ho's *Liquidated: An Ethnography of Wall Street*
Geert Hofstede's *Culture's Consequences: Comparing Values, Behaviors, Institutes and Organizations across Nations*
Claude Lévi-Strauss's *Structural Anthropology*
Jay Macleod's *Ain't No Makin' It: Aspirations and Attainment in a Low-Income Neighborhood*
Saba Mahmood's *The Politics of Piety: The Islamic Revival and the Feminist Subject*
Marcel Mauss's *The Gift*

BUSINESS

Jean Lave & Etienne Wenger's *Situated Learning*
Theodore Levitt's *Marketing Myopia*
Burton G. Malkiel's *A Random Walk Down Wall Street*
Douglas McGregor's *The Human Side of Enterprise*
Michael Porter's *Competitive Strategy: Creating and Sustaining Superior Performance*
John Kotter's *Leading Change*
C. K. Prahalad & Gary Hamel's *The Core Competence of the Corporation*

CRIMINOLOGY

Michelle Alexander's *The New Jim Crow: Mass Incarceration in the Age of Colorblindness*
Michael R. Gottfredson & Travis Hirschi's *A General Theory of Crime*
Richard Herrnstein & Charles A. Murray's *The Bell Curve: Intelligence and Class Structure in American Life*
Elizabeth Loftus's *Eyewitness Testimony*
Jay Macleod's *Ain't No Makin' It: Aspirations and Attainment in a Low-Income Neighborhood*
Philip Zimbardo's *The Lucifer Effect*

ECONOMICS

Janet Abu-Lughod's *Before European Hegemony*
Ha-Joon Chang's *Kicking Away the Ladder*
David Brion Davis's *The Problem of Slavery in the Age of Revolution*
Milton Friedman's *The Role of Monetary Policy*
Milton Friedman's *Capitalism and Freedom*
David Graeber's *Debt: the First 5000 Years*
Friedrich Hayek's *The Road to Serfdom*
Karen Ho's *Liquidated: An Ethnography of Wall Street*

The Macat Library By Discipline

John Maynard Keynes's *The General Theory of Employment, Interest and Money*
Charles P. Kindleberger's *Manias, Panics and Crashes*
Robert Lucas's *Why Doesn't Capital Flow from Rich to Poor Countries?*
Burton G. Malkiel's *A Random Walk Down Wall Street*
Thomas Robert Malthus's *An Essay on the Principle of Population*
Karl Marx's *Capital*
Thomas Piketty's *Capital in the Twenty-First Century*
Amartya Sen's *Development as Freedom*
Adam Smith's *The Wealth of Nations*
Nassim Nicholas Taleb's *The Black Swan: The Impact of the Highly Improbable*
Amos Tversky's & Daniel Kahneman's *Judgment under Uncertainty: Heuristics and Biases*
Mahbub Ul Haq's *Reflections on Human Development*
Max Weber's *The Protestant Ethic and the Spirit of Capitalism*

FEMINISM AND GENDER STUDIES

Judith Butler's *Gender Trouble*
Simone De Beauvoir's *The Second Sex*
Michel Foucault's *History of Sexuality*
Betty Friedan's *The Feminine Mystique*
Saba Mahmood's *The Politics of Piety: The Islamic Revival and the Feminist Subject*
Joan Wallach Scott's *Gender and the Politics of History*
Mary Wollstonecraft's *A Vindication of the Rights of Woman*
Virginia Woolf's *A Room of One's Own*

GEOGRAPHY

The Brundtland Report's *Our Common Future*
Rachel Carson's *Silent Spring*
Charles Darwin's *On the Origin of Species*
James Ferguson's *The Anti-Politics Machine*
Jane Jacobs's *The Death and Life of Great American Cities*
James Lovelock's *Gaia: A New Look at Life on Earth*
Amartya Sen's *Development as Freedom*
Mathis Wackernagel & William Rees's *Our Ecological Footprint*

HISTORY

Janet Abu-Lughod's *Before European Hegemony*
Benedict Anderson's *Imagined Communities*
Bernard Bailyn's *The Ideological Origins of the American Revolution*
Hanna Batatu's *The Old Social Classes And The Revolutionary Movements Of Iraq*
Christopher Browning's *Ordinary Men: Reserve Police Batallion 101 and the Final Solution in Poland*
Edmund Burke's *Reflections on the Revolution in France*
William Cronon's *Nature's Metropolis: Chicago And The Great West*
Alfred W. Crosby's *The Columbian Exchange*
Hamid Dabashi's *Iran: A People Interrupted*
David Brion Davis's *The Problem of Slavery in the Age of Revolution*
Nathalie Zemon Davis's *The Return of Martin Guerre*
Jared Diamond's *Guns, Germs & Steel: the Fate of Human Societies*
Frank Dikotter's *Mao's Great Famine*
John W Dower's *War Without Mercy: Race And Power In The Pacific War*
W. E. B. Du Bois's *The Souls of Black Folk*
Richard J. Evans's *In Defence of History*
Lucien Febvre's *The Problem of Unbelief in the 16th Century*
Sheila Fitzpatrick's *Everyday Stalinism*

The Macat Library By Discipline

Eric Foner's *Reconstruction: America's Unfinished Revolution, 1863-1877*
Michel Foucault's *Discipline and Punish*
Michel Foucault's *History of Sexuality*
Francis Fukuyama's *The End of History and the Last Man*
John Lewis Gaddis's *We Now Know: Rethinking Cold War History*
Ernest Gellner's *Nations and Nationalism*
Eugene Genovese's *Roll, Jordan, Roll: The World the Slaves Made*
Carlo Ginzburg's *The Night Battles*
Daniel Goldhagen's *Hitler's Willing Executioners*
Jack Goldstone's *Revolution and Rebellion in the Early Modern World*
Antonio Gramsci's *The Prison Notebooks*
Alexander Hamilton, John Jay & James Madison's *The Federalist Papers*
Christopher Hill's *The World Turned Upside Down*
Carole Hillenbrand's *The Crusades: Islamic Perspectives*
Thomas Hobbes's *Leviathan*
Eric Hobsbawm's *The Age Of Revolution*
John A. Hobson's *Imperialism: A Study*
Albert Hourani's *History of the Arab Peoples*
Samuel P. Huntington's *The Clash of Civilizations and the Remaking of World Order*
C. L. R. James's *The Black Jacobins*
Tony Judt's *Postwar: A History of Europe Since 1945*
Ernst Kantorowicz's *The King's Two Bodies: A Study in Medieval Political Theology*
Paul Kennedy's *The Rise and Fall of the Great Powers*
Ian Kershaw's *The "Hitler Myth": Image and Reality in the Third Reich*
John Maynard Keynes's *The General Theory of Employment, Interest and Money*
Charles P. Kindleberger's *Manias, Panics and Crashes*
Martin Luther King Jr's *Why We Can't Wait*
Henry Kissinger's *World Order: Reflections on the Character of Nations and the Course of History*
Thomas Kuhn's *The Structure of Scientific Revolutions*
Georges Lefebvre's *The Coming of the French Revolution*
John Locke's *Two Treatises of Government*
Niccolò Machiavelli's *The Prince*
Thomas Robert Malthus's *An Essay on the Principle of Population*
Mahmood Mamdani's *Citizen and Subject: Contemporary Africa And The Legacy Of Late Colonialism*
Karl Marx's *Capital*
Stanley Milgram's *Obedience to Authority*
John Stuart Mill's *On Liberty*
Thomas Paine's *Common Sense*
Thomas Paine's *Rights of Man*
Geoffrey Parker's *Global Crisis: War, Climate Change and Catastrophe in the Seventeenth Century*
Jonathan Riley-Smith's *The First Crusade and the Idea of Crusading*
Jean-Jacques Rousseau's *The Social Contract*
Joan Wallach Scott's *Gender and the Politics of History*
Theda Skocpol's *States and Social Revolutions*
Adam Smith's *The Wealth of Nations*
Timothy Snyder's *Bloodlands: Europe Between Hitler and Stalin*
Sun Tzu's *The Art of War*
Keith Thomas's *Religion and the Decline of Magic*
Thucydides's *The History of the Peloponnesian War*
Frederick Jackson Turner's *The Significance of the Frontier in American History*
Odd Arne Westad's *The Global Cold War: Third World Interventions And The Making Of Our Times*

The Macat Library By Discipline

LITERATURE

Chinua Achebe's *An Image of Africa: Racism in Conrad's Heart of Darkness*
Roland Barthes's *Mythologies*
Homi K. Bhabha's *The Location of Culture*
Judith Butler's *Gender Trouble*
Simone De Beauvoir's *The Second Sex*
Ferdinand De Saussure's *Course in General Linguistics*
T. S. Eliot's *The Sacred Wood: Essays on Poetry and Criticism*
Zora Neale Huston's *Characteristics of Negro Expression*
Toni Morrison's *Playing in the Dark: Whiteness in the American Literary Imagination*
Edward Said's *Orientalism*
Gayatri Chakravorty Spivak's *Can the Subaltern Speak?*
Mary Wollstonecraft's *A Vindication of the Rights of Women*
Virginia Woolf's *A Room of One's Own*

PHILOSOPHY

Elizabeth Anscombe's *Modern Moral Philosophy*
Hannah Arendt's *The Human Condition*
Aristotle's *Metaphysics*
Aristotle's *Nicomachean Ethics*
Edmund Gettier's *Is Justified True Belief Knowledge?*
Georg Wilhelm Friedrich Hegel's *Phenomenology of Spirit*
David Hume's *Dialogues Concerning Natural Religion*
David Hume's *The Enquiry for Human Understanding*
Immanuel Kant's *Religion within the Boundaries of Mere Reason*
Immanuel Kant's *Critique of Pure Reason*
Søren Kierkegaard's *The Sickness Unto Death*
Søren Kierkegaard's *Fear and Trembling*
C. S. Lewis's *The Abolition of Man*
Alasdair MacIntyre's *After Virtue*
Marcus Aurelius's *Meditations*
Friedrich Nietzsche's *On the Genealogy of Morality*
Friedrich Nietzsche's *Beyond Good and Evil*
Plato's *Republic*
Plato's *Symposium*
Jean-Jacques Rousseau's *The Social Contract*
Gilbert Ryle's *The Concept of Mind*
Baruch Spinoza's *Ethics*
Sun Tzu's *The Art of War*
Ludwig Wittgenstein's *Philosophical Investigations*

POLITICS

Benedict Anderson's *Imagined Communities*
Aristotle's *Politics*
Bernard Bailyn's *The Ideological Origins of the American Revolution*
Edmund Burke's *Reflections on the Revolution in France*
John C. Calhoun's *A Disquisition on Government*
Ha-Joon Chang's *Kicking Away the Ladder*
Hamid Dabashi's *Iran: A People Interrupted*
Hamid Dabashi's *Theology of Discontent: The Ideological Foundation of the Islamic Revolution in Iran*
Robert Dahl's *Democracy and its Critics*
Robert Dahl's *Who Governs?*
David Brion Davis's *The Problem of Slavery in the Age of Revolution*

Alexis De Tocqueville's *Democracy in America*
James Ferguson's *The Anti-Politics Machine*
Frank Dikotter's *Mao's Great Famine*
Sheila Fitzpatrick's *Everyday Stalinism*
Eric Foner's *Reconstruction: America's Unfinished Revolution, 1863-1877*
Milton Friedman's *Capitalism and Freedom*
Francis Fukuyama's *The End of History and the Last Man*
John Lewis Gaddis's *We Now Know: Rethinking Cold War History*
Ernest Gellner's *Nations and Nationalism*
David Graeber's *Debt: the First 5000 Years*
Antonio Gramsci's *The Prison Notebooks*
Alexander Hamilton, John Jay & James Madison's *The Federalist Papers*
Friedrich Hayek's *The Road to Serfdom*
Christopher Hill's *The World Turned Upside Down*
Thomas Hobbes's *Leviathan*
John A. Hobson's *Imperialism: A Study*
Samuel P. Huntington's *The Clash of Civilizations and the Remaking of World Order*
Tony Judt's *Postwar: A History of Europe Since 1945*
David C. Kang's *China Rising: Peace, Power and Order in East Asia*
Paul Kennedy's *The Rise and Fall of Great Powers*
Robert Keohane's *After Hegemony*
Martin Luther King Jr.'s *Why We Can't Wait*
Henry Kissinger's *World Order: Reflections on the Character of Nations and the Course of History*
John Locke's *Two Treatises of Government*
Niccolò Machiavelli's *The Prince*
Thomas Robert Malthus's *An Essay on the Principle of Population*
Mahmood Mamdani's *Citizen and Subject: Contemporary Africa And The Legacy Of Late Colonialism*
Karl Marx's *Capital*
John Stuart Mill's *On Liberty*
John Stuart Mill's *Utilitarianism*
Hans Morgenthau's *Politics Among Nations*
Thomas Paine's *Common Sense*
Thomas Paine's *Rights of Man*
Thomas Piketty's *Capital in the Twenty-First Century*
Robert D. Putman's *Bowling Alone*
John Rawls's *Theory of Justice*
Jean-Jacques Rousseau's *The Social Contract*
Theda Skocpol's *States and Social Revolutions*
Adam Smith's *The Wealth of Nations*
Sun Tzu's *The Art of War*
Henry David Thoreau's *Civil Disobedience*
Thucydides's *The History of the Peloponnesian War*
Kenneth Waltz's *Theory of International Politics*
Max Weber's *Politics as a Vocation*
Odd Arne Westad's *The Global Cold War: Third World Interventions And The Making Of Our Times*

POSTCOLONIAL STUDIES

Roland Barthes's *Mythologies*
Frantz Fanon's *Black Skin, White Masks*
Homi K. Bhabha's *The Location of Culture*
Gustavo Gutiérrez's *A Theology of Liberation*
Edward Said's *Orientalism*
Gayatri Chakravorty Spivak's *Can the Subaltern Speak?*

The Macat Library By Discipline

PSYCHOLOGY

Gordon Allport's *The Nature of Prejudice*
Alan Baddeley & Graham Hitch's *Aggression: A Social Learning Analysis*
Albert Bandura's *Aggression: A Social Learning Analysis*
Leon Festinger's *A Theory of Cognitive Dissonance*
Sigmund Freud's *The Interpretation of Dreams*
Betty Friedan's *The Feminine Mystique*
Michael R. Gottfredson & Travis Hirschi's *A General Theory of Crime*
Eric Hoffer's *The True Believer: Thoughts on the Nature of Mass Movements*
William James's *Principles of Psychology*
Elizabeth Loftus's *Eyewitness Testimony*
A. H. Maslow's *A Theory of Human Motivation*
Stanley Milgram's *Obedience to Authority*
Steven Pinker's *The Better Angels of Our Nature*
Oliver Sacks's *The Man Who Mistook His Wife For a Hat*
Richard Thaler & Cass Sunstein's *Nudge: Improving Decisions About Health, Wealth and Happiness*
Amos Tversky's *Judgment under Uncertainty: Heuristics and Biases*
Philip Zimbardo's *The Lucifer Effect*

SCIENCE

Rachel Carson's *Silent Spring*
William Cronon's *Nature's Metropolis: Chicago And The Great West*
Alfred W. Crosby's *The Columbian Exchange*
Charles Darwin's *On the Origin of Species*
Richard Dawkin's *The Selfish Gene*
Thomas Kuhn's *The Structure of Scientific Revolutions*
Geoffrey Parker's *Global Crisis: War, Climate Change and Catastrophe in the Seventeenth Century*
Mathis Wackernagel & William Rees's *Our Ecological Footprint*

SOCIOLOGY

Michelle Alexander's *The New Jim Crow: Mass Incarceration in the Age of Colorblindness*
Gordon Allport's *The Nature of Prejudice*
Albert Bandura's *Aggression: A Social Learning Analysis*
Hanna Batatu's *The Old Social Classes And The Revolutionary Movements Of Iraq*
Ha-Joon Chang's *Kicking Away the Ladder*
W. E. B. Du Bois's *The Souls of Black Folk*
Émile Durkheim's *On Suicide*
Frantz Fanon's *Black Skin, White Masks*
Frantz Fanon's *The Wretched of the Earth*
Eric Foner's *Reconstruction: America's Unfinished Revolution, 1863-1877*
Eugene Genovese's *Roll, Jordan, Roll: The World the Slaves Made*
Jack Goldstone's *Revolution and Rebellion in the Early Modern World*
Antonio Gramsci's *The Prison Notebooks*
Richard Herrnstein & Charles A Murray's *The Bell Curve: Intelligence and Class Structure in American Life*
Eric Hoffer's *The True Believer: Thoughts on the Nature of Mass Movements*
Jane Jacobs's *The Death and Life of Great American Cities*
Robert Lucas's *Why Doesn't Capital Flow from Rich to Poor Countries?*
Jay Macleod's *Ain't No Makin' It: Aspirations and Attainment in a Low Income Neighborhood*
Elaine May's *Homeward Bound: American Families in the Cold War Era*
Douglas McGregor's *The Human Side of Enterprise*
C. Wright Mills's *The Sociological Imagination*

Thomas Piketty's *Capital in the Twenty-First Century*
Robert D. Putman's *Bowling Alone*
David Riesman's *The Lonely Crowd: A Study of the Changing American Character*
Edward Said's *Orientalism*
Joan Wallach Scott's *Gender and the Politics of History*
Theda Skocpol's *States and Social Revolutions*
Max Weber's *The Protestant Ethic and the Spirit of Capitalism*

THEOLOGY

Augustine's *Confessions*
Benedict's *Rule of St Benedict*
Gustavo Gutiérrez's *A Theology of Liberation*
Carole Hillenbrand's *The Crusades: Islamic Perspectives*
David Hume's *Dialogues Concerning Natural Religion*
Immanuel Kant's *Religion within the Boundaries of Mere Reason*
Ernst Kantorowicz's *The King's Two Bodies: A Study in Medieval Political Theology*
Søren Kierkegaard's *The Sickness Unto Death*
C. S. Lewis's *The Abolition of Man*
Saba Mahmood's *The Politics of Piety: The Islamic Revival and the Feminist Subject*
Baruch Spinoza's *Ethics*
Keith Thomas's *Religion and the Decline of Magic*

COMING SOON

Chris Argyris's *The Individual and the Organisation*
Seyla Benhabib's *The Rights of Others*
Walter Benjamin's *The Work Of Art in the Age of Mechanical Reproduction*
John Berger's *Ways of Seeing*
Pierre Bourdieu's *Outline of a Theory of Practice*
Mary Douglas's *Purity and Danger*
Roland Dworkin's *Taking Rights Seriously*
James G. March's *Exploration and Exploitation in Organisational Learning*
Ikujiro Nonaka's *A Dynamic Theory of Organizational Knowledge Creation*
Griselda Pollock's *Vision and Difference*
Amartya Sen's *Inequality Re-Examined*
Susan Sontag's *On Photography*
Yasser Tabbaa's *The Transformation of Islamic Art*
Ludwig von Mises's *Theory of Money and Credit*

Macat Disciplines

Access the greatest ideas and thinkers across entire disciplines, including

FEMINISM, GENDER AND QUEER STUDIES

Simone De Beauvoir's
The Second Sex

Michel Foucault's
History of Sexuality

Betty Friedan's
The Feminine Mystique

Saba Mahmood's
The Politics of Piety: The Islamic Revival and the Feminist Subject

Joan Wallach Scott's
Gender and the Politics of History

Mary Wollstonecraft's
A Vindication of the Rights of Woman

Virginia Woolf's
A Room of One's Own

Judith Butler's
Gender Trouble

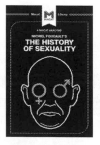

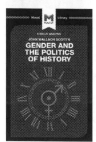

Macat Disciplines

Access the greatest ideas and thinkers across entire disciplines, including

INEQUALITY

Ha-Joon Chang's, *Kicking Away the Ladder*
David Graeber's, *Debt: The First 5000 Years*
Robert E. Lucas's, *Why Doesn't Capital Flow from Rich To Poor Countries?*
Thomas Piketty's, *Capital in the Twenty-First Century*
Amartya Sen's, *Inequality Re-Examined*
Mahbub Ul Haq's, *Reflections on Human Development*

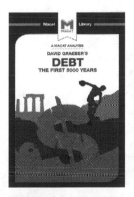
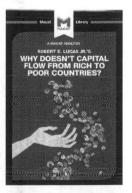

Macat analyses are available from all good bookshops and libraries.

Access hundreds of analyses through one, multimedia tool.
Join free for one month **library.macat.com**

Macat Disciplines

*Access the greatest ideas and thinkers
across entire disciplines, including*

CRIMINOLOGY

Michelle Alexander's
*The New Jim Crow:
Mass Incarceration in the
Age of Colorblindness*

**Michael R. Gottfredson
& Travis Hirschi's**
A General Theory of Crime

Elizabeth Loftus's
Eyewitness Testimony

**Richard Herrnstein
& Charles A. Murray's**
*The Bell Curve: Intelligence and
Class Structure in American Life*

Jay Macleod's
*Ain't No Makin' It:
Aspirations and Attainment in a
Low-Income Neighborhood*

Philip Zimbardo's
The Lucifer Effect

Macat Disciplines

Access the greatest ideas and thinkers across entire disciplines, including

Macat Pairs

*Analyse historical and modern issues
from opposite sides of an argument.
Pairs include:*

HOW TO RUN AN ECONOMY

John Maynard Keynes's
*The General Theory OF Employment,
Interest and Money*

Classical economics suggests that market economies
are self-correcting in times of recession or depression,
and tend toward full employment and output. But
English economist John Maynard Keynes disagrees.

In his ground-breaking 1936 study *The General
Theory*, Keynes argues that traditional economics
has misunderstood the causes of unemployment.
Employment is not determined by the price of labor;
it is directly linked to demand. Keynes believes market
economies are by nature unstable, and so require
government intervention. Spurred on by the social
catastrophe of the Great Depression of the 1930s,
he sets out to revolutionize the way the world thinks

Milton Friedman's
The Role of Monetary Policy

Friedman's 1968 paper changed the course of
economic theory. In just 17 pages, he demolished
existing theory and outlined an effective alternate
monetary policy designed to secure 'high employment,
stable prices and rapid growth.'

Friedman demonstrated that monetary policy plays
a vital role in broader economic stability and argued
that economists got their monetary policy wrong
in the 1950s and 1960s by misunderstanding the
relationship between inflation and unemployment.
Previous generations of economists had believed
that governments could permanently decrease
unemployment by permitting inflation—and vice versa.
Friedman's most original contribution was to show that
this supposed trade-off is an illusion that only works in
the short term.

Macat analyses are available from all good bookshops and libraries.

Access hundreds of analyses through one, multimedia tool.
Join free for one month **library.macat.com**

Macat Disciplines

Access the greatest ideas and thinkers across entire disciplines, including

THE FUTURE OF DEMOCRACY

Robert A. Dahl's, *Democracy and Its Critics*
Robert A. Dahl's, *Who Governs?*
Alexis De Toqueville's, *Democracy in America*
Niccolò Machiavelli's, *The Prince*
John Stuart Mill's, *On Liberty*
Robert D. Putnam's, *Bowling Alone*
Jean-Jacques Rousseau's, *The Social Contract*
Henry David Thoreau's, *Civil Disobedience*

Macat Disciplines

Access the greatest ideas and thinkers across entire disciplines, including

TOTALITARIANISM

Sheila Fitzpatrick's, *Everyday Stalinism*
Ian Kershaw's, *The "Hitler Myth"*
Timothy Snyder's, *Bloodlands*

Macat Pairs

Analyse historical and modern issues from opposite sides of an argument. Pairs include:

RACE AND IDENTITY

Zora Neale Hurston's
Characteristics of Negro Expression

Using material collected on anthropological expeditions to the South, Zora Neale Hurston explains how expression in African American culture in the early twentieth century departs from the art of white America. At the time, African American art was often criticized for copying white culture. For Hurston, this criticism misunderstood how art works. European tradition views art as something fixed. But Hurston describes a creative process that is alive, ever-changing, and largely improvisational. She maintains that African American art works through a process called 'mimicry'—where an imitated object or verbal pattern, for example, is reshaped and altered until it becomes something new, novel—and worthy of attention.

Frantz Fanon's
Black Skin, White Masks

Black Skin, White Masks offers a radical analysis of the psychological effects of colonization on the colonized.

Fanon witnessed the effects of colonization first hand both in his birthplace, Martinique, and again later in life when he worked as a psychiatrist in another French colony, Algeria. His text is uncompromising in form and argument. He dissects the dehumanizing effects of colonialism, arguing that it destroys the native sense of identity, forcing people to adapt to an alien set of values—including a core belief that they are inferior. This results in deep psychological trauma.

Fanon's work played a pivotal role in the civil rights movements of the 1960s.

Macat analyses are available from all good bookshops and libraries.

Access hundreds of analyses through one, multimedia tool.
Join free for one month **library.macat.com**

Macat Pairs

*Analyse historical and modern issues
from opposite sides of an argument.
Pairs include:*

INTERNATIONAL RELATIONS IN THE 21ST CENTURY

Samuel P. Huntington's
The Clash of Civilisations

In his highly influential 1996 book, Huntington offers a vision of a post-Cold War world in which conflict takes place not between competing ideologies but between cultures. The worst clash, he argues, will be between the Islamic world and the West: the West's arrogance and belief that its culture is a "gift" to the world will come into conflict with Islam's obstinacy and concern that its culture is under attack from a morally decadent "other."

Clash inspired much debate between different political schools of thought. But its greatest impact came in helping define American foreign policy in the wake of the 2001 terrorist attacks in New York and Washington.

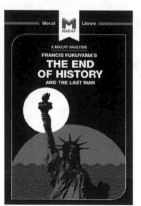

Francis Fukuyama's
The End of History and the Last Man

Published in 1992, *The End of History and the Last Man* argues that capitalist democracy is the final destination for all societies. Fukuyama believed democracy triumphed during the Cold War because it lacks the "fundamental contradictions" inherent in communism and satisfies our yearning for freedom and equality. Democracy therefore marks the endpoint in the evolution of ideology, and so the "end of history." There will still be "events," but no fundamental change in ideology.

Macat Disciplines

Access the greatest ideas and thinkers across entire disciplines, including

MAN AND THE ENVIRONMENT

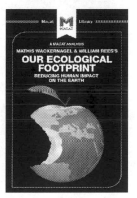

The Brundtland Report's, *Our Common Future*
Rachel Carson's, *Silent Spring*
James Lovelock's, *Gaia: A New Look at Life on Earth*
Mathis Wackernagel & William Rees's, *Our Ecological Footprint*

Macat analyses are available from all good bookshops and libraries.

Access hundreds of analyses through one, multimedia tool.
Join free for one month **library.macat.com**

Macat Pairs

Analyse historical and modern issues from opposite sides of an argument. Pairs include:

ARE WE FUNDAMENTALLY GOOD - OR BAD?

Steven Pinker's
The Better Angels of Our Nature

Stephen Pinker's gloriously optimistic 2011 book argues that, despite humanity's biological tendency toward violence, we are, in fact, less violent today than ever before. To prove his case, Pinker lays out pages of detailed statistical evidence. For him, much of the credit for the decline goes to the eighteenth-century Enlightenment movement, whose ideas of liberty, tolerance, and respect for the value of human life filtered down through society and affected how people thought. That psychological change led to behavioral change—and overall we became more peaceful. Critics countered that humanity could never overcome the biological urge toward violence; others argued that Pinker's statistics were flawed.

Philip Zimbardo's
The Lucifer Effect

Some psychologists believe those who commit cruelty are innately evil. Zimbardo disagrees. In *The Lucifer Effect*, he argues that sometimes good people do evil things simply because of the situations they find themselves in, citing many historical examples to illustrate his point. Zimbardo details his 1971 Stanford prison experiment, where ordinary volunteers playing guards in a mock prison rapidly became abusive. But he also describes the tortures committed by US army personnel in Iraq's Abu Ghraib prison in 2003—and how he himself testified in defence of one of those guards. committed by US army personnel in Iraq's Abu Ghraib prison in 2003—and how he himself testified in defence of one of those guards.

Macat analyses are available from all good bookshops and libraries.

Access hundreds of analyses through one, multimedia tool.

Join free for one month **library.macat.com**

Macat Pairs

Analyse historical and modern issues from opposite sides of an argument. Pairs include:

HOW WE RELATE TO EACH OTHER AND SOCIETY

Jean-Jacques Rousseau's
The Social Contract

Rousseau's famous work sets out the radical concept of the 'social contract': a give-and-take relationship between individual freedom and social order.

If people are free to do as they like, governed only by their own sense of justice, they are also vulnerable to chaos and violence. To avoid this, Rousseau proposes, they should agree to give up some freedom to benefit from the protection of social and political organization. But this deal is only just if societies are led by the collective needs and desires of the people, and able to control the private interests of individuals. For Rousseau, the only legitimate form of government is rule by the people.

Robert D. Putnam's
Bowling Alone

In *Bowling Alone*, Robert Putnam argues that Americans have become disconnected from one another and from the institutions of their common life, and investigates the consequences of this change.

Looking at a range of indicators, from membership in formal organizations to the number of invitations being extended to informal dinner parties, Putnam demonstrates that Americans are interacting less and creating less "social capital" – with potentially disastrous implications for their society.

It would be difficult to overstate the impact of *Bowling Alone*, one of the most frequently cited social science publications of the last half-century.

Printed in the United States
by Baker & Taylor Publisher Services